NOTHING OVER THE SIDE

OTHER BOOKS BY Dr RAY SOLLY

Supertanker: Anatomy and Operation
Picturesque Harbours
Gravesend: A History of Your Town
Mariner's Launch
BP Shipping: A Group Fleet History (Co-author)
Mariner's Voyage
Athel Line: A Fleet History
Manual of Tanker Operations (Co-author)
Tanker: The History and Development of Crude Oil Tankers (In preparation)
Mariner's Rest (In preparation)

NOTHING OVER THE SIDE

EXAMINING SAFE CRUDE OIL TANKERS

Dr Ray Solly

Whittles Publishing

Published by
Whittles Publishing,
Dunbeath,
Caithness KW6 6EY,
Scotland, UK

www.whittlespublishing.com

ISBN 978-1904445-94-4

Printed by InPrint, Latvia

Contents

Well researched and presented books on the sea provide a wealth of information about ships and the operations they undertake. This book investigates and reports on the author's experiences on board a range of crude oil tankers and provides a valuable insight into the complex operations of such vessels, as well as the way systems have developed to ensure that they meet the exacting regulations imposed upon their operators.

Although Dr Solly's book is about ships and shipping and is of direct relevance to the shipping industry, it is also a book for non-maritime personnel who rely more than they realise upon refined oil products for the activities which they take for granted in today's modern world.

The book provides a thought-provoking and informative read, and a thorough record of tanker operations today.

Gary Hindmarch C.Eng

Head of Marine College, South Tyneside College

Preface

As an ex-VLCC deck officer, reading journalistic books and witnessing ongoing media reports over the years criticising crude oil tankers, developed my interest in these ships, but fired also a sense of injustice. Conversations with the International Association of Independent Tanker Owners (Intertanko) and ship owners confirmed the generally held belief that the crude oil carrier rarely receives a favourable press and that a more balanced representation might be conceivable. It was agreed that a couple of short haul voyages could prove useful enabling a non-journalist to ask searching questions about operational tankers and enabling an unbiased book—the only work of its type—to be written.

Subsequent experiences updated my knowledge and made me increasingly aware of the competency and concerns for safety shown by seafarers working these essential ships, their owners/managers, and those involved at ports and jetties. I met dedicated professionalism at all levels, and left believing the operation of crude oil tankers to be among the most regulated industries in the world.

I received considerably more cooperation than expected. My research uncovered numerous political, social, environmental and statutory issues too extensive for examination at sea, which required discussions with authorities ashore augmented by a range of maritime reading. These subsequent investigations determined issues too complex to be examined thoroughly within the limitations of a non-specialist author using the confines of a short book. However, I felt I could offer the shipping industry and other interested readers (that should include all of us) an enhanced awareness by merely giving an airing to such important concerns.

I sincerely hope that the book proves interesting and informative to whoever reads it.

Ray Solly

ACKNOWLEDGEMENTS

This book would not have been possible without considerable help and assistance from a number of authoritative and influential organisations who arranged and made possible two up-dating voyages, and permitted meetings with executives to discuss the issues examined. I am indeed grateful to them for their efforts, and to the Master, officers and crew of each *British Ensign* and *Anna Knutsen*. The opinions expressed however are entirely from my own deliberations and in no way represent viewpoints of any organisation mentioned.

Amongst those who offered assistance: Intertanko, BP Shipping, Knutsen OAS, International Maritime Organisation, International Association of Classification Societies, Oil Companies International Marine Forum, Tanker Structure Co-Operative Forum, Lloyds, International Chamber of Shipping, Department of Transport, Nautilus International, International Shipping Federation, Institute of Marine Engineering, Science and Technology, Clarkson PLC, Braemar Seascope Limited. Lloyds Ship Manager, Telegraph, Tanker Operator, Fairplay, Motor Ship, Journal of The Honourable Company of Master Mariners, Seaways.

Introduction

Autumn dampness seeped through my elbow-sleeves as I leant on the wooden bridge-rail aboard BP Shipping's 36,713-tonne summer-deadweight (s-dwt) motor tanker mt *British Ensign*. Two very large crude carriers in Europoort Terminal on our port side appeared impressively solid as our ship increased to a safe speed out of Rotterdam. I was on board for a two-week voyage observing and updating my knowledge of ship management and operating techniques. The trip followed ten days on Knutsen OAS of Norway's 129,154 s-dwt shuttle tanker, mt *Anna Knutsen*, during which I had gained insight into North

The shuttle tanker *Anna Knutsen* lies gently at her berth in Tranmere South oil jetty. This photograph was taken in the late 1990s prior to the fitting of additional anti-pollution devices and long before a round voyage aboard her became a possibility (Author's Collection).

Sea oil carrying. This trade was totally new to me, but with Knutsen's managing the largest fleet of these specialist ships in the world, the company had proved an excellent starting point. As an ex-supertanker navigating officer conveying crude oil around various oceans of the world in vast quantities, I was able to appreciate the inherent gracefulness in these vessels, but was also acutely aware of inherent dangers.

Cocooned in the isolated safety of ships, immersed in daily routines of uneventful voyages, I had failed to register properly the vital role crude oil tankers play in the lives of the world's civilised population. Only since leaving the sea had I reached a more focussed and heightened awareness of the crucial importance of these ships in our lives. It seems that all developed countries possess insatiable appetites for crude products, a singular fact that elevates tankers to an essential role in modern existence. The extent to which each one of us, whatever our age and condition, depends totally on oil and has close—even intimate—involvement with this industry proved a sobering thought. Consumption of fuel by cars is the most prominent use for many people but it is far from our only need for oil. We are all-embracing consumers of petrol and diesel fuels for air, sea, land and rail transport; in our homes, businesses and industries. Refined products are basic to the manufacture of many commodities and have colossal impact on everyday living. Crude oil tankers are the specialist vessels designed, managed and operated purely to carry this cargo in its elemental form to our refineries and are instrumental in ensuring such consumable necessities remain available to satisfy our needs. Yet I was equally aware that, proportionally to their importance, these vessels represent only a minute part of the massive resources involved in oil production, marketing and sales.

There are two circumstances when people universally think about tankers. The first, which has never happened, could occur were tankers to cease trading. The second happened for a brief period in 2008 over parts of the United Kingdom when petrol at the pumps dried up for a two-day period during a road-tanker drivers' dispute. This created major problems at some petrol stations, caused a mini-crisis in most of the country's supermarkets, and struck panic in virtually all of the nation's car drivers and lorry owners. It led to the government rapidly formulating plans for military intervention to keep essential services running. Fortunately, the dispute was settled—because it was recognised that it had to be—before that wider-reaching state developed.

Another occasion also rarely occurs. All the time oil stays in the ship there is little need for focus on the vessel and how it operates. No-one (least of all an 'ex-tanker type') would deny that crude oil carriers have had their share of accidents resulting in environmental disasters of truly horrific enormity. All oil cargoes are potentially dangerous, but my trips aboard *Anna Knutsen* and *British Ensign* had increased my awareness that the transportation industry has made great strides to control effectively its side of the wider business. Reading a technical journal had recently confirmed that crude oil tankers account for very little worldwide sea pollution. Figures from ITOPF (The International Tanker Owners Pollution Federation) indicate that less than 2% of such pollution arises from accidents or incidents. Listening to the world's media it seems that the greatest pollution of our oceans—and of the air, for that matter—comes from international industrial waste.

Although I had been contented in teaching, over the intervening years restless thoughts had strayed frequently to my time spent at sea. These moments were invariably fired by seeing crude oil carriers from my balcony on passage through the south-west shipping lane in the Dover Strait and—inevitably—visualising the navigating officer taking his watch, and *living* what he was doing at that moment on board his vessel. On each sighting, my enthusiasm was fired anew and

I felt that old familiar urge to 'make just one more voyage' to find out for myself how much things had altered across a range of areas since my own seagoing days. The two short-haul passages had resulted; I believed they would help me see for myself what was happening aboard today's oil tankers and, in the process, update and enhance my professional awareness and knowledge.

It seemed, in the light of the importance of the product to the 'man in the street', that others might share my quest for knowledge about this ubiquitously complex industry of significant proportions. After all, thousands of men and ships move millions of tonnes of crude around the globe every day. It seemed surely that insight into what actually occurs on board and some knowledge of how these ships are navigated, operated and managed might be of paramount importance to a great many thinking people.

BP Shipping Company's tanker *British Ensign* lies alongside her fitting-out berth prior to ballasting and sailing on her maiden voyage. This versatile handy-sized tanker was designed to carry a range of cargoes covering petroleum products, and was fitted with a specially strengthened hull equipping her to operate in ice waters (BP Shipping).

My ship-borne observations on *Anna Knutsen* showed how considerably things had moved ahead since I had 'swallowed the anchor', for already insight had been gained into the ways such tankers today *are* safely managed and controlled, efficiently run and economically viable. I had witnessed procedures involving

Vessels navigating with caution through thick ice in the Baltic Sea. The pressures against the hull in the vicinity of the waterline are considerable as the ships proceed on passage in lanes often created by specially designed ice-breakers (V. Volden).

operations on deck, in the engine-room and on the bridge, and seen how recent cargo regulations had practically advanced oil transportation. My BP Shipping voyage confirmed, consolidated and enhanced these findings, but left me feeling there were still many questions of interest to all thinking people which remained unanswered.

The realistic thought had occurred even before I set out on my first voyage that my delving might leave me 'fobbed off' with a host of smooth responses. I arrived on the ships equipped with some technical knowledge and know-how and was prepared to stiffen my resolve, take on board whatever I witnessed, uncover any obvious deficiencies, and not to whitewash that which would be recorded. As it happened, I had been permitted to wander around *Anna Knutsen* unhindered, and most of my questions had been answered in detail, so it had not proved necessary for my background sympathies to bias observations of the shipboard practices made as I examined initiatives creating such reliable ships. I had gained insight into some wider legal issues colouring occurrences aboard the vessel, particularly current thoughts about ballast water transference, sea/air pollution control, and crew recruitment, along with ship constructional concerns and actions from disreputable owners and indifferent flag-state service practitioners which unfortunately bring the entire industry into disrepute. I felt, however, that I would have to seek ashore for more detailed information, but waited to see what would transpire from a second voyage with a totally different tanker operator.

As both ships ploughed through North Sea waters, an additional interesting thought crossed my mind. Most people ashore—including the families of many seafarers—have no idea what happens aboard crude oil carriers, which is after all the workplace of their loved ones. The professional activities of husband, son/daughter or father, or even next-door neighbour, remain a complete mystery.

I was aware of a further popular but weak belief. To most people ashore all classes of tanker are lumped together and sometimes painted with the same brush. In the horrific stories of the *Erika* and *Prestige*, for example, ships which had caused considerable pollution within EU territorial waters before becoming embroiled in an international furore, the vessels were known merely as 'tankers'. In fact, neither of these was carrying crude oil, for both were product ships. Whilst considering tankers as a generic group, it is interesting to remember that hundreds of

The supertanker *Front Duchess* lies at her berth in Europoort's Petroleumhaven that was designed specifically for partially-laden crude oil carriers of maximum 400,000 s-dwt tonnage. This 286,000 s-dwt tanker was built in 1993 and is owned by Frontline Shipping Company of Oslo (Author's Collection).

Officers and crew undertaking normal duties in the wheel-house of a large tanker (V. Volden).

closely regulated chemical and gas carriers also navigate our seas daily in perfect safety.

So, as I leant reflectively on the bridge rail aboard *British Ensign* while we sailed majestically out of Europoort, it seemed that the continuance of my task remained not only interesting and exciting, but really quite daunting.

CHAPTER 1

A New Trade and a Few Surprises

When I sailed aboard the *Anna Knutsen* the ship was a shuttle tanker engaged on short sea voyages transporting crude oil from various North Sea oilfields to refineries mainly on the Continent and in the United Kingdom. The vessel has subsequently reverted to deep-sea trading. She was launched in 1987 at the Wartsila shipyard in Finland, and completed in Fredrikstad as a purpose-built 129,154 s-dwt (summer deadweight tonnage) shuttle tanker, fitted with two controllable-pitch propellers

Anna Knutsen lying alongside her berth at Tranmere North Oil Jetty taking voluntary part in a port operation exercise. The tanker has completed discharge and has been ballasted prior to her return voyage for further loading (Knutsen OAS).

and two bow thrusters for greater manoeuvrability. She was of 69,313 gross registered tons (grt). The tanker was constructed with double bottom or lower double hull, ten cargo tanks, plus two for oil 'slops', the residue from tank cleaning, along with safety devices of inert gas system, crude oil washing facilities, and ballast tanks segregated from the cargo. In 2004 she went to Gdansk to have watertight bulkheads built into those wing cargo tanks near the ship's plating, thus creating a void space and coming as close as practicable to turning her (in effect) into a 'double-hulled and sided' tanker.

Oil production from the North Sea began during the 1970s, following the first oil strike in November 1969 when Phillips Petroleum made a major find in the Ekofisk field in the Norwegian sector. Further major discoveries included BP's Forties field and the Brent field discovered by Shell and Esso. It was to exploit North Sea oil developments that the need arose for a new type of vessel—the specialist shuttle tanker. These were fitted with bow-loading facilities to enable development of a unique type of cargo-loading technique, which could lift crude oil from deepwater single-point mooring installations or Floating Production, Storage and Offloading (FPSO) vessels moored in offshore oilfields. They were equipped with gas flaring systems to burn off unwanted fractions and could partly process crude oil. Most FPSOs are converted tankers of about 100,000 s-dwt, although some shipyards offer standard design purpose-built ships. It was the demand for FPSOs that had prompted several owners, including Knutsen OAS, to convert older single-hull tankers, which might otherwise have become redundant under new regulations governing the phase-out of single-hull ships. The trade was new to me and I hoped, during my voyage, to witness practical navigational and seamanship operations germane to all tankers, as well of course as those relating to the shuttle trade. Additionally, the prospect of going away to sea—admittedly in an observer's rather than a more actively

An impressive duo of shots showing a large tanker owned by a leading ship-owner made fast to a Floating Production, Storage and Offloading (FPSO) vessel by day and by night (P. Harrington).

professional role—was exciting and I looked forward to being on board ship again.

Security at oil refineries in the United Kingdom and most terminals worldwide has always been strict to the point of severity. Taxis or private cars rarely travel inside the perimeter fence and it remains mandatory for seafarers and visitors to show official permits stating reasons for visiting, supported by photographic identification, to security guards at the gate before boarding minibuses to make the transit to tanker jetties. When lengthy distances (perhaps as much as a quarter of a mile) still remain, deep-sea gear, ship's stores and replacement equipment can be pushed on the four-wheeled trolleys provided. As inevitably happens on occasions, larger items of replacement equipment are transferred from a motor barge using the ship's lifting gear, but the replacement of other items (such as the fitting of a spare anchor) would be done only during a statutory dry-docking. From the refinery entrance I could see the impressive black and red funnel and contrasting white superstructure of *Anna Knutsen* as she lay quietly alongside her berth at Tranmere North jetty.

Halfway along the access road, our driver inserted a swipe card that allowed entry through a massive iron gate. Safely deposited on the other side with my gear I noticed the ship was starboard side to her berth and slightly down by the stern. I guessed she had completed discharge and was stripping or draining tanks prior to ballasting operations necessary to bring her on to an even keel, submerging bulbous bow, rudder and propeller. Lugging my gear, I climbed the structure supporting the gangway leading to the main deck and pressed the security buzzer enabling the duty AB (able seaman) on board to release the inside gangway catch by remote control.

In the seconds crossing between shore and ship, I glanced at the broad expanse of red main deck. Immediately recognisable were cargo manifolds connecting the pipe systems of the tanker with Chiksans® (or rigid crane arms) leading to storage tanks

Steps leading to the security gate and gangway can be seen, along with the arms of the Chiksan connection between cargo tank and refinery. The duty Able Seaman is just visible by the gangway. The safe walkway is a legal requirement permitting an unencumbered path fore and aft (Author's Collection).

ashore. The white of the vast accommodation block contrasted strongly with coloured decking and red cautionary notices reinforcing the traditional tanker no-smoking rule. The duty AB and another member of the crew were conspicuous in bright orange gear, with luminous white facings, white hard hats, gloves and heavy-duty shoes, a rig that was to me something of a novelty. I recognised major items of ship's gear such as the IGS (inert gas system) on the port side, the catwalk for safe passage in heavy seas, and the run of service pipes extending the length of the deck. I noticed another pipe running from port side aft into the raised superstructure on the fo'c'sle head, which

I assumed to be the forward oil-loading pipeline from the cargo buoy. A tower on the starboard side near the gangway was not immediately recognisable and I wondered vaguely at the function of this equipment.

The duty AB smiled a cautious welcome as he confirmed my identity, commenting, 'Ah—you must be our writer chap, sir', leaving me slightly nonplussed. He checked my passport details against a printed sheet and asked for a signature before taking my gear and leading me towards the impressive superstructure. Entering the safety double doors leading to the companionway, he slipped blue plastic covers over his deck shoes to protect lino and carpets before we took the lift to Number One poop deck. Here I met the Norwegian senior officers: the master, Captain Eirik Angell, and his chief engineer. Their welcome was cordial, but I detected an air of caution as we entered the Master's office and he also compared my passport details against information supplied from Knutsen OAS's head office at Haugesund in Norway. He then allowed me to send emails to my wife advising my arrival on board and confirming 'all was well' and afterwards, over a coffee, we relaxed in each other's company. It was during this chat that I learnt the reasons for my apparently guarded reception. Head office had outlined the purpose of my visit, but with previously adverse publications about their industry foremost in the captain's and officers' minds they were naturally curious to find precisely my expectations and discover how these might influence my stay as a guest in their ship. That I had served at sea aboard crude oil tankers some years previously proved useful and enabled familiarity with the processes and procedures associated with seafaring. As the Master advised later, my presence on board was soon regarded as 'user friendly'. Officers and ratings on this ship were all Norwegian, apart from a Swedish electrician. The chief engineer had served aboard British registered tankers earlier in his career. The ship carried also a party of seven Polish painters who worked on board for six-monthly periods engaged on maintenance and upkeep of most deck areas, external accommodation and internal working parts of the ship. These duties were outside the capacity of the 21-man crew who were required for other specialised duties.

Captain Angell introduced me to the chief officer seated in front of a computer in the cargo control room which, on all shuttle tankers, is fully computerised. Use of keyboards and screens permit control and monitoring of all operations involving

The VOC monitoring cabinet showing screen saver (Author's Collection).

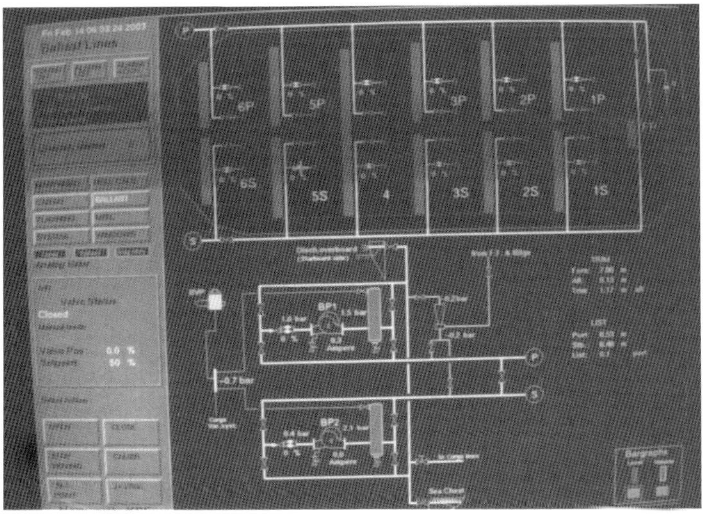

A mimic diagram showing the ballast pump and lines aboard a shuttle tanker covering the range of tanks and compartments served by the segregated ballast system which operates totally independently of the cargo lines (V. Volden).

loading and discharging of cargo and ballasting, including crude oil washing of tanks on a rotation basis. The state of all cargo tanks, including ullages (the height between the top of the cargo and underside of deck) and temperatures may be seen at a glance, along with tank bottom and deck lines. He was opening sea cocks in the engine-room and commencing ballasting by

The 7.4-metre-long lifeboat has a capacity of thirty persons, which means it can take all of the crew and offer protection from both sea and the worst extremes of weather. Crew-members would each wear lifejackets, survival suits and safety equipment, whilst the boat was fully provisioned and fitted with electronic detection apparatus enabling quick identification of its position by search and rescue craft. Officers and crew sat facing aft, towards and under the instruction of the safety officer in charge of the boat, who faced forward (Author's Collection).

allowing tonnes of the Mersey to enter the segregated ballast tanks (SBTs) with their independent pump system, isolated from cargo handling facilities. The senior second mate also on duty was instructed to take me to Number One deck and rig me out with a temporary set of the safety gear worn by all crew, mandatory before proceeding on deck.

I related quickly to both officers and liked the relaxed yet single-minded purposefulness as they performed their duties. On deck, a safety brief followed, concerning action I should take in the event of any emergency, including appropriate alarm signals, and I was informed my station would be in the wheelhouse with the captain to await further instructions. We then adjourned to the single stern-launched covered lifeboat on its davit where my seat was indicated.

Unpacking my gear in the Owner's Cabin on Number Four poop deck I reflected on immediate impressions. My cordial, friendly reception helped me relax as I set out my gear in the roomy cabin, and sorted notes and background material necessary for my various lines of enquiry. The furnishing of the Owner's cabin was to a high standard with fittings representative of the excellent accommodation provided by the Company for all officers and ratings. Cabins were roomy, comfortable and adequate for the purposes provided. A second wardrobe was fitted on the opposite of the entrance,

It was all too soon in the voyage that I found mountains of research material and work that needed exploration–and explanation–as I settled back to seafaring routines (Authors' Collection).

5. Safety regulations

5.1 Obligation to follow safety regulations

Safety is our highest priority. An accident will not only affect yourself, but also your family. In addition, accidents and injuries affect our future business opportunities. The award by taking a short cut is therefore far less than the risk of something going wrong. **Remember there is always enough time for safe execution. Breach of safety regulations will result in a warning. Dismissal will be the final consequence in case of repeated breaches. A serious breach may result in immediate dismissal.**

We expect you to report if you observe defect equipment or irregularities that you may suspect represent a safety hazard. Only by right safety attitudes and by being alert we shall be able to meet our safety targets.

5.2 Non conformities

All accidents have a cause. If something happens, the "root cause" should be found. Such causes may be:

- The work place is not safe (lack of stagings, light and ventilation)
- Safety equipment is not used
- Lack of sleep or training
- Improper tools and work description.

It is only possible to avoid same things happen again by identification of the root cause. Minor non-conformities shall be discussed and rectified onboard, while more important ones shall be reported to the head office on a "Quality Reporting Form" (QRF). Recommended improvements will then be reviewed and implemented on other ships as well.

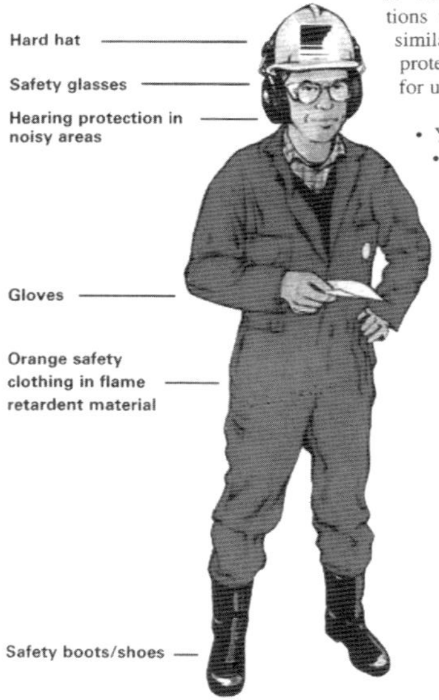

5.3 Personal Safety

On arrival onboard for the first time you will receive a set of personal safety equipment. You should take well care of it. Only when it is worn out you will receive a new set.

Approved safety equipment shall be worn at all times on deck and in the engine room, as well as in the Cargo Control Room.

Hard hats with chin straps shall always be worn when working at other locations than in the accommodation and similar areas. On chemical tankers eye protection shall be fitted on helmets for use on deck. Be aware that

- Your vision cannot be restored
- Noise may reduce your hearing capabilities for the rest of your life

When you work with chemicals additional protection is required. Read the data sheets of the product to be used and take the necessary precautions. Filter masks are kept in the custody of the department heads, who make sure that correct filters are used and that the masks are in proper condition. It is our policy that if protection is required in a cargo tank, only breathing apparatus shall be used.

Dust masks shall be used as required.

An extract from the introductory pamphlet and safety handbook fastened in an appropriate wallet to the back of all cabin doors. This section indicates the considerable unequivocal emphasis placed by the Company on all aspects of personal safety (Knutsen OAS).

and officer's cabins were supplied with comfortable armchairs, settees and a large coffee table.

My eye was caught by a 24-page *Safety Handbook* in a cellophane envelope fixed to the cabin bulkhead. This served as both an introduction to the ship and as a personal safety pamphlet and proved a veritable mine of information for Knutsen's seafarers, whether established or new to the profession, and both marine and non-maritime visitors. The booklet provided basic details of safety and emergency regulations, ship organisation, maintenance, and safety functions associated with specialised operations such as helicopter transportation, crane and mooring operations.

Increases in shipboard safety and terminal security were not the only differences observed from my previous seafaring, for I soon became aware of the emphasis on personnel safety with warning notices around the ship, and the non-self-conscious wearing by all crew members of the deck safety gear necessary aboard tankers. Conforming to existing legislation was taken by

All crew-members shared a common saloon for meals. The senior officers' table was at the top right-hand corner, whilst the door to the left led into a comfortable joint officer-crew lounge equipped with large screen television and video. Incorporated into the suite was a small library and games room, with separate computer facilities including email (Author's Collection).

everyone in their stride as a purely natural process. All ranks and ratings observed safety regulations in wearing approved equipment before venturing onto the main deck.

My first dinner with the Master, chief engineer and chief officer was at the senior officers' table in the saloon. Aboard Norwegian ships, officers and ratings ate all meals in the same saloon simultaneously, but with their own separate tables for officers, petty officers and crew.

Outside the dining room entrance a senior officers' general and off-duty area was provided where not only coffee could be enjoyed, but a chance afforded for socialising and relaxing between periods of duty. All Knutsen tankers remain 'dry ships' for no alcohol is carried or consumed on board (Author's Collection).

At the senior table, we enjoyed service from one of two stewardesses whilst other crew-members used a cafeteria system. Female stewards were very much a novelty both to me and aboard British vessels, but their employment aboard Scandinavian ships had been a normal procedure for many years and seemed to work well. The messing also was a far cry from the British system where ratings ate in a separate mess, but I was far from convinced of the success of the Norwegian method. This was not from any snobbish perspective, for I noticed during all meals an air of reserved control in the stilted conversations around me. Officers and ratings were far more monosyllabic than I remembered aboard other ships and their chat lacked that spontaneous flow and relaxed laughter previously associated with meals aboard vessels where a two-saloon system operated. Officers and ratings shared also the same mess room equipped with television, video and computers, although outside the saloon was a small area fitted with two comfortable settees where senior officers met for coffee mornings, afternoons and after meals, and relaxed at occasional moments during the day.

Sitting quietly in my cabin after dinner, I reviewed questions raised in my mind by these first hours on *Anna Knutsen*. Along with those already prepared before joining the ship, others flooded my mind concerning the development of current safety practices introduced since my previous service aboard a crude oil tanker. I was interested particularly in the way operational techniques worked on such a specialist ship, in their efficiency, and in the progress made over preceding years in computerised systems of cargo control, navigation and communications. I recognised there was much for me to learn.

Just after midnight—the estimated time of departure from Tranmere—I went up one deck to the wheelhouse and joined the two pilots, Master and junior second officer. Subdued chart-table working lights contrasted strongly with powerful lamps from jetty and forepart posts. The latter flooded the main deck with a harsh glare that reflected off the bright red paintwork, emphasising the starkness of piping and equipment. Seen from the 215.9-metre distance from bridge to bow, the figures of the crew forward working under supervision of the senior chief officer seemed diminutive as they singled up by letting go warps not completely necessary to keep the tanker to her berth. We still held a head-rope and back spring, and had made fast our forward tug, whose three white masthead lights were just visible off the port bow in the clear but dark night. The junior chief officer was in charge on the after-deck and had similarly singled up and taken his tug.

Mooring arrangements forward, aft and along the main deck. At first glance, the tonnages may appear inadequate for such a large ship that, at her Summer Draught working load line, displaces 147,339 metric tonnes until it is remembered that dead weights are handled more easily in water than air (Knutsen OAS).

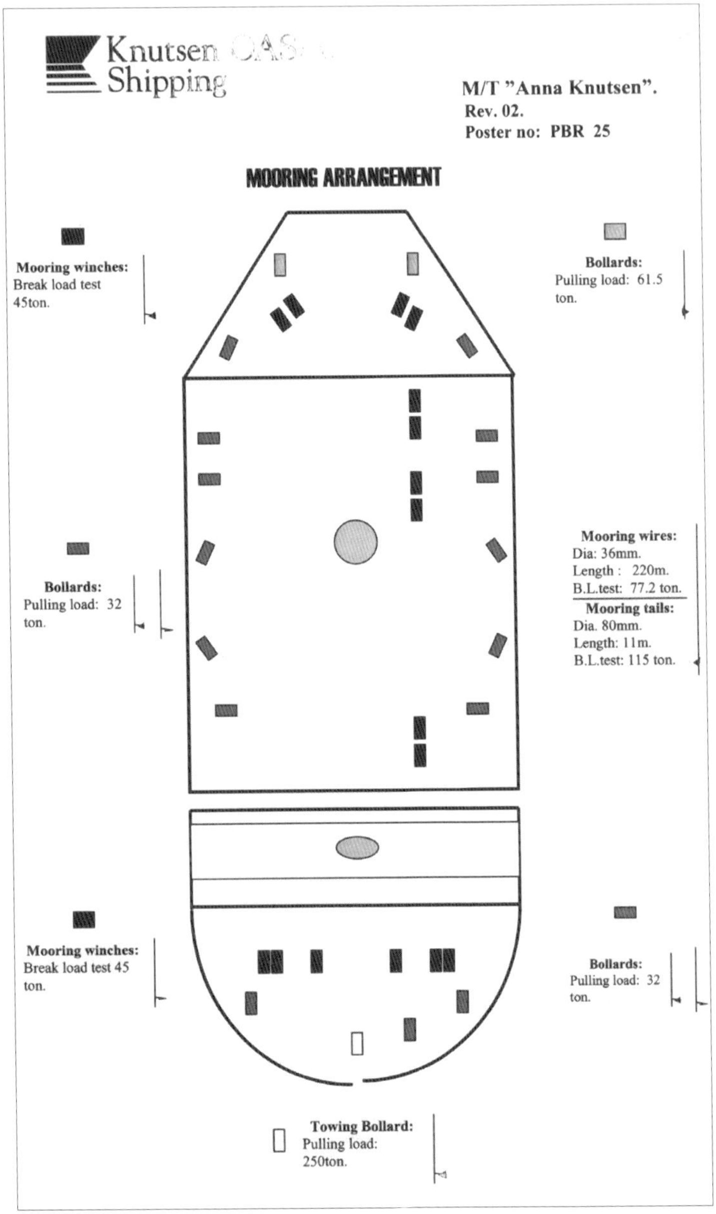

In the wheelhouse, our 10-cm and 3-cm radars were tuned and operational, whilst the apprentice-AB quietly attended the wheel. Both fully computerised radars were of the open-viewing type that enabled more than one person to examine the Plan Position Indicators (PPIs; pictures painted by computer graphics onto the physical screen from the raw radar input). Two radars were carried that were interchangeable between available ranges. This was not merely in case one 'crashed', although that was important, but because each operated on a separate wavelength (10 cm and 3 cm respectively), they detected various targets more effectively relative to range and responses. Both were set to True Motion, North-Up display, offering a gull's eye view of the coast in relation to the ship that assisted navigation, and of the shipping situation for the range in use. Windows situated at the lower part of the screen on the 10-cm radar belonged to ARPA (Automatic Radar Plotting Aid). They provided computerised collision-avoidance data and gave at a glance the closest approach distance and time between our ship and a potential target. The system automatically calculated and

The three screens on the top left-hand side of the photograph indicate the flat screen daylight viewing radars of the type carried aboard all merchant ships. One each covers the 10cm and 3cm displays with windows offering a range of selected information including collision avoidance data. The third screen is linked to the chart and shows the position of the ship relative to its surroundings (Author's Collection).

plotted vessels as they appeared on the radar screen and gave course projections, indicating risk of collision where this existed. Proposed alterations to ones' own vessel's manoeuvres could also be assessed before taking action.

I noticed other things new to me: a checklist with the various tasks for departing from port clearly defined, showing haphazard ticks indicating the second mate had acknowledged these duties immediately upon completion. Lying at an angle slightly hidden below this was a copy of the company safety leaflet indicating procedures for taking and letting go harbour escort tugs. It was obvious both instructions for safety were being taken seriously. Above the chart-table, with the *River Mersey* and *Port of Liverpool Approaches* charts prepared and parallel rules and sharpened pencils placed ready near the logbook, the computerised chart system was setup, showing the tanker's position. The Master advised that this particular equipment was experimental but to date had proved extremely reliable. The quietly authoritative voices of senior pilot and master discussed finer points of the departure plan, whilst the second officer stood by to transmit the first telegraph and helm orders. The familiarity of the scene was strongly reminiscent of my own days acting as third officer in the wheelhouse during any standby before promotion.

With a sudden burst of movement, the deck lights were switched off and both pilots, accompanied by the master, crossed to the starboard-side bridge-wing in preparation for bringing *Anna Knutsen* off her berth into the Mersey. With all fore and aft warps let go and winched in, the tugs took the strain of this 257-metre long tanker and, following instructions received via the vhf from the senior pilot, gently nudged her from the berth before turning the ship through 180 degrees until the bows faced downstream. Once she was centred up, as the Master and senior pilot looked carefully around to confirm

Knutsen OAS Shipping

M/T "ANNA KNUTSEN"

VOYAGE WAYPOINT PLAN

Voyage Number:	962/06	**Draft Fwd**	**6.50**
Voyage Plan Number:	17	**Draft Mid**	**7.50**
Port of Departure:	Tranmere	**Draft Aft**	**8.50**
Port of Destination:	Statfjord		
Estimated Date & Time of Departure:	01.08.06 02:00		
Estimated Date & Time of Arrival at speed:	13.00 **kts**	03.08.06 07:06	

Charts for the voyage:
BA:3490-1951-1978-1826-1411-2093- 2198- 2199-2798-2723-2722-1796-1795-1794-1785-2720-1954-1119-294-295 (2 & 4140)
Short description of the voyage: 1942
In ballast from Tranmere to Statfjord.

	WP No	WP Name	Lat.	Long.	Water depth mtr.	UKC mtr.	Course	Dist.	Sailed dist.	Dist. to go	ETA to WP	Remarks	Pos. fix Intervals
1	17	Liverpool Pilot	N 53 31.5	W 003 20.5	18	9.5				677.4		Bar l/f in 330* dist. 0.6 n.m.	
2	18	Liverpool Bay	N 53 33.5	W 003 40.0	32	23.5	280°	11.8	11.8	665.6	01.08.06 02:54	GPS POS: N53*33.5' W003*40'	
3	15	Chicken Rock	N 54	W 004 55.0	40	31.5	301°	51.6	63.4	614.0	01.08.06 06:52	Chicken Rock in 050* dist. 3.7 n.m.	
4	19	Mew Island North	N 54 43.7	W 005 21.8	126	117.5	340°	46.4	109.8	567.6	01.08.06 10:26	Mew Island in 251* dist. 5.5 n.m.	
5	20	Mull of Kintyre	N 55 16.8	W 005 52.2	111	102.5	332°	37.4	147.2	530.2	01.08.06 13:19	Mull of Kintyre in 064* dist. 2.7 n.m.	
6	21	Altacarry NE.	N 55 24.9	W 006 02.6	100	91.5	324°	10.0	157.2	520.1	01.08.06 14:05	Altacarry Head in 213* dist. 8.2 n.m.	
7	22	N. Of Rathlin Island	N 55 26.3	W 006 14.1	98	89.5	282°	6.7	163.9	513.5	01.08.06 14:36	Altacarry Head in 165* dist.8.5 n.m	
8	23	Rhinns of Islay.	N 55 47.3	W 006 58.3	45	36.5	310°	32.6	196.5	480.8	01.08.06 17:07	GPS POS: N55*47.3' W 006*58.3'	
9	9	Skerry Vore	N 56 14.5	W 007 31.0	125	116.5	326°	32.8	229.3	448.1	01.08.06 19:38	Skerry Vore in 071* dist. 14.3 n.m.	
10	24	Neist Point	N 57 27.9	W 006 52.3	163	154.5	016°	76.4	305.7	371.7	02.08.06 01:30	Neist Point in 134* dist. 3.7 n.m.	
11	25	Waternish Point	N 57 38.4	W 006 39.1	130	121.5	034°	12.7	318.4	359.0	02.08.06 02:29	Waternish Point in 163* dist. 2.0 n.m.	
12	26	Eilean Trodday	N 57 44.9	W 006 16.2	67	58.5	062°	13.9	332.2	345.1	02.08.06 03:33	Eilean Trodday in 212* dist. 1.5 n.m.	
13	27	Rubha Reidh	N 57 50.8	W 006 05.2	100	91.5	045°	8.3	340.5	336.8	02.08.06 04:11	GPS POS : N 57*50.8' W 006*05.2'	
14	28	Cape Wrath	N 58 42.0	W 005 05.5	62	53.5	032°	60.1	400.6	276.8	02.08.06 08:48	Cape Wrath in 146* dist. 5.1 n.m.	
15	29	Sule Skerry	N 59	W 004 23.0	71	62.5	051°	28.4	429.0	248.4	02.08.06 11:00	Sule skerr in 352* dist. 4.9 n.m.	
16	30	North Shoal	N 59 17.8	W 003 54.5	115	106.5	039°	23.0	452.0	225.3	02.08.06 12:46	GPS POS : N 59* 17,8' W 003* 54.5'	
17	359	Mull Head	N 59 31.8	W 003 01.0	72	63.5	063°	30.6	482.6	194.7	02.08.06 15:07		
18	360	Dennis Head	N 59 31.8	W 002 20.0	71	62.5	090°	20.8	503.4	173.9	02.08.06 16:43	N of Dennis Head, Fair Isle Ch eastward	
19	361	S of Fair Isle	N 59 16.2	W 001 42.0	75	66.5	129°	24.9	528.3	149.1	02.08.06 18:38		
20	2	Statfjord 10 N.M. Z SW.	N 61 08.0	E 001 36.5	138	129.5	041°	149.1	677.4	0.0	03.08.06 06:06	Brent "C" in 123* dist 4.1 n.m.	
21													
22													
23													
24													
25													
26													
27													
28													
29													
30													
31													
32													
33													
34													
35													
36													
37													
38													
39													
40													
									Total	677.4	N. Miles		

Voyage Waypoint Plan prepared before departure indicating points of the trip where major alterations to course occur. Such plans are always provisional: this one for instance was amended due to unforeseen weather circumstances that led to dropping the pilot at Lynas Point, off the north Welsh coast, rather than at the planned pilotage station off the Bar Light vessel, twelve miles outside the Liverpool buoyed channel (Knutsen OAS).

Liverpool port control's advice via their Vessel Tracking Service (VTS) that other shipping had been advised of our movements and the way was clear, both tugs were let go and, with one in attendance aft but not made fast, the tanker gradually increased speed to steerage way and commenced her outward passage.

It was then the Master gave me a copy of the Voyage Plan detailing intended passage arrangements for the trip towards Statfjord Oil Field in the North Sea. This conglomerate of three platforms and two buoys lies just north of our UK Brent Field, which led Captain Angell to give me a sidelong glance as he said that the Norwegians were tapping into our field in order to supplement their own reserves. I responded to his tongue-in-cheek teasing by affecting astonishment and, keeping a straight face, advised that my own information led me to believe we had been tapping into theirs 'for some years now', and I hoped that 'both countries never managed to cross their pipes—otherwise we might each end up with our own oil back'. His smiled response led the pilots also to contribute appropriate quips—about 'the *entente cordiale* being well oiled'. It was interesting, that whilst these exchanges were happening, our eyes constantly and instinctively took in everything occurring in the wheelhouse, such as the tanker's position and courses being steered by the apprentice, to movements of shipping and the state of the river generally. Being back on the bridge of a ship was like fitting my hand into a well-worn glove.

After we had dropped the pilots at Point Lynas, instead of the Bar Light vessel owing to increasingly heavy weather, the senior second officer (rested after his sleep) took the bridge watch from the junior second. As we altered course northwards, the tanker plunged into a moderate Force Six gusting Eight north-westerly. I felt myself doing a sort of *pas de deux* across the wheelhouse as the ballasted ship plunged into rough seas and moderate swell off her port bow. Grabbing the support bar to the radar, I

Even large oil tankers are affected by heavy seas and high swell. Severe weather up to Gale Force 8 gusting 9 or Storm Force 10 are not uncommon on ordinary sea-going passages in virtually any sea-way out of the lee of the land. When fully laden, these ships pitch and roll only moderately, but the stresses on the hull are considerable (V. Volden).

watched as heavy spray from forward splashed halfway along the main deck. The tanker adopted a corkscrew motion, which although uncomfortable, did not leave me feeling seasick. In extremely severe conditions, ships sometimes reduced speed to prevent pounding, or even increase speed, to desynchronise the length/speed ratio proportional to the wavelength. In Storm Force Ten conditions of 60-plus miles per hour winds can whip up waves to 20 or more metres—with troughs extending one third the length of a ship—conditions that would have grounded aircraft and resulted in ferries remaining in harbour. Tankers in such circumstances are expected to keep going and arrive at their destination regardless of adverse conditions experienced on passage. Delay off the refinery could mean disrupting tight schedules and probably losing the berth to another vessel, leading to an inevitable lying at anchor for a few days—with corresponding loss in revenue—and potential disruption at the petrol pump. When in ballast conditions, crude oil tankers could flood selected cargo tanks with seawater in order to lower the centres of gravity and buoyancy and so create a more stable platform. When I asked the Master about this, he informed me that *Anna Knutsen* kept Numbers 3 Centre and 2 Wings cargo tanks for such use in heavy weather as safety measure ballasting, with the former being filled to 58% capacity and the latter to 70%. Although this ship experienced frequent North Sea storms, it was only on rare occasions that use was made of this emergency measure. Even so, this same ship had in January 2004 received repair to her bottom plating resulting from slamming damage sustained from heavy seas.

The 687-nautical-mile trip took three days until *Anna Knutsen* approached the ten-mile end-of-sea-passage zone before slowing down for arrival off the submerged loading pipeline. I spent much of this passage on the bridge and around the ship talking to officers and crew and finding Norwegian shipboard fun and humour differed little from that experienced aboard other vessels. Watchkeeping on the bridge held few surprises and it was easy to follow navigational and collision avoidance practices. I was impressed by the AIS (or Automatic Identification System) based on Global Positioning System (GPS) that allowed immediate identification of most other vessels sighted. This equipment permitted bridge officers to identify most targets detected by radar and allowed verbal contact to be made where necessary if intentions might not be immediately clear so helping avoid collision by professional discussion. Knutsen officers, in keeping with the majority of those on the bridge of 99% of coastal and deep-sea ships, do not consciously dwell on possibilities of collision and stranding. Aware these incidents can happen during any close-quarter situation, they make professional assessments aided by thorough training and experience and invariably initiate remedial action that reduces risks to a minimum. Collisions and stranding do not occur every day. The last time any supertanker (crude oil carrier in excess of 160,000 s-dwt on the London Freight brokers' Average Freight Rate Assessment (AFRA) Fixed scale, or over 200,000 s-dwt on the Flexible Market scale) experienced serious incident was in 1989 when *Exxon Valdez* grounded in Prince William Sound.

Numerous routine deck work activities are undertaken during calm weather whilst the tanker is under way. Much of this includes painting of deck and accommodation areas or even the routine task of cleaning wheel-house windows and the wiper blades (V. Volden).

Opportunity also occurs during ordinary passage making to maintain, make repairs or adjustments to bridge and other equipment. Here plans are consulted before action is taken to rectify a minor fault occurring in bridge gear (V. Volden).

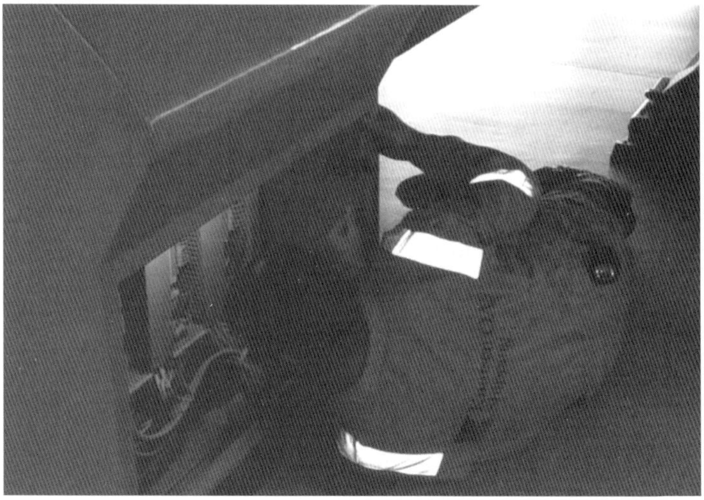

As is true of any professional ashore or afloat, it is dangerously unhealthy to focus too much on 'what might happen'. In such reflective mode, whilst 'mashing' a round of tea, I noticed three waste bins by the side of the after locker, one used to capture general trash that was burnt in the ship's incinerator, the others intended to receive paper and plastic bottles for offloading and recycling ashore.

Donning my deck gear during this passage, I joined the crew on deck making minor adjustments to equipment and

Helicopter operations are routines aboard all tankers, and other ships for that matter, usually involving the transference of personnel or stores. Regulations governing the landing are complied with strictly and it is rare today for incidents to occur that might result in injury or worse (V. Volden).

doing inevitable servicing of moving parts of deck equipment. We spent some time attending the starboard-side 21-metre deck crane that had (in the manner of gremlins common aboard any ship) managed to turn her runner 'into a bunch of knitting', as I described the muddled wire confronting us to the bosun supervising his crew on deck, much to his amusement. The cause was clear: when last used the wire had crossed its track whilst being reeled in and, in the melee of events at the time, this had passed unnoticed. The incident was minor, took a few minutes only to sort out, but stood as 'one of those incidents' which happen aboard any ship—or in any other domain ashore—where equipment relies upon human beings for its operation. Whilst observing our crew working on the manifold area I noted that fuel oil and vapour lines were duplicated fore and aft between the four main cargo manifolds served by the cargo pumps. A moment's thought revealed the logic in this, for it enabled access to these pipes on occasions when access might be blocked by cross-pipes or terminal obstruction. The vapour lines would be used only in some ports (such as Liverpool Bay,

I was informed) to prevent the smell of oil fumes contaminating the environment and proving offensive to local residents.

Much time was spent in the Master's conference room delving into operating books, manuals and plans, and talking to the engineering officers and mates updating my knowledge, and learning more about shuttle tanker techniques. My research encompassed statutory documents held on board all International Maritime Organization (IMO) ships including Safety of Life at Sea (SOLAS) and Prevention of Pollution at Sea (MARPOL) manuals and Standards of Training, Certification and Watchkeeping (STCW) documents. Of most of these, I possessed some acquaintance, but I took the opportunity to update my knowledge of numerous international booklets covering helicopter operations, oil spillage prevention and mooring guides, International Ship Management Codes, Bridge Procedures, and Crude Oil Washing (COW) regulations. There was a mountain of reading, including numerous amendments, with which all watch-keeping officers had to retain familiarisation.

Safety aboard tankers today owes much to legislation originating from the mid-1990s when the International Safety Management (ISM) Code was implemented for tankers, bulk carriers and certain other ships. This came into force in July 1998 and required companies to have clear lines of command and responsibility, which were subject to auditing and certification by registered flag states. Requirements governing the training and certification of crew were revised under 1995 and subsequent Amendments to the STCW Convention. This required owners to gauge competence of their crews according to new criteria, and ensure crew qualifications were internationally recognised. New rules also came into effect governing minimum and maximum hours of work and rest for crew-members.

Anna Knutsen was fitted with a double bottom of 2.5 metres' depth upon building but had been retrofitted in December 2004 at a Polish shipyard with an oil-tight bulkhead two metres inside the single hull to create void tanks that separated cargo in Numbers 2A, 2B, 4 and 6 Wing tanks port and starboard from the ship's sides. Number 1, 3 and 5 port and starboard were permanent water-ballast tanks. This special dry-docking sandwiched between the statutory inspections had converted the tanker effectively into 'a double-hulled ship'. The conversion was an ingenious strategy that made a positive contribution towards preventing environmental pollution in the event of collision—at the expense of payload. The tanker was due her next annual dry dock a few months later.

It was during this trip to Statfjord that I mentioned to the chief officer and engineer the 'mysterious tower' noticed whilst boarding the ship in Tranmere. Observing the completion of ballast in the computerised cargo control room, I had noticed an adjacent cabinet indicating the current performance of 'VOC equipment'. He informed me that the cabinet and tower represented technology to reduce the emission of gases that pollute the atmosphere, and resulted from Annex VI of IMO Regulations governing Air Pollution. VOC stands for 'volatile organic compounds' and is a generic term for hydrocarbon compounds found in crude oil. On board ship, this mixes with an inert gas taken from funnel exhausts, which following a complicated process of cleaning, is pumped into empty or half-full cargo tanks to exclude oxygen and help prevent risks of explosion. During loading, riser pipes pump this mixture into the atmosphere. Ships are far from being the only culprits. When all of us—on every occasion—as the 'international man in the street' fill the huge numbers of cars we own collectively with petrol at the pump, we release damaging hydrocarbon gases into our atmosphere. Contributions—in *vast* quantities—come from other non-marine sources, such as aircraft, lorries, factories, waste disposal plants as well of course as millions of industrial processes, which often incorporate additional use

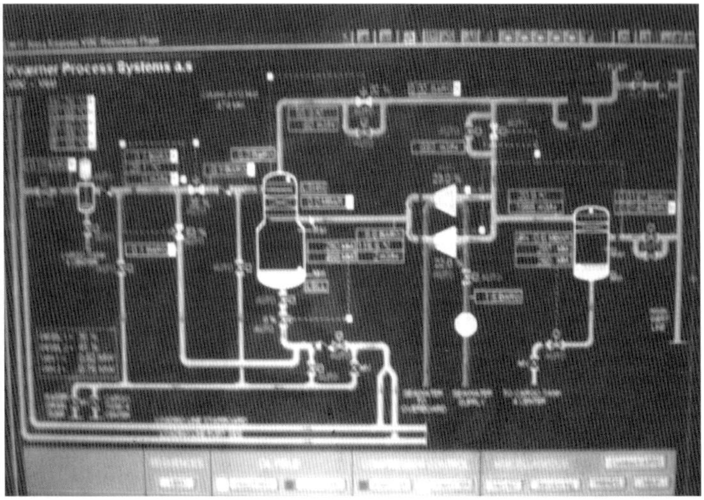

The Volatile Organic Compounds (VOC) cabinet in the cargo control room indicates levels and performance at all stages of operation and when on stand-by (Author's Collection).

Views (right and facing) looking from aft and forward of the VOC deck equipment fitted to *Anna Knutsen* as an integral part of controlling air pollution from the mixture of hydrocarbon and inert gases in the cargo tanks vented during loading of crude oil. Instead of rising into the open air, the non-methane mixture is recovered (Author's Collection).

of solvents and additives. Our own homes also must share an element of responsibility for such emissions. These gases are damaging, for close to the ground they can transform into 'near-ground ozone', which is carcinogenic. Aboard tankers, the problem to personnel is not great because crew only see the commodity they are transporting whilst physically taking samples and measuring ullages. It is rare today to open tanks whilst on passage because computerised tank radars regularly monitor ullages and oil temperatures and display any required results continuously on screens in the cargo control room and elsewhere.

All shuttle tanker operators involved in the responsible efforts to find solutions are faced with some complicated difficulties. Crude oil contains elements of methane gas, known as Liquid Natural Gas (LNG), which proves difficult to recover and requires highly expensive specialised cooling plants to reduce it to the temperature of −162°C necessary for it to liquidise at atmospheric pressure. Reasons of cost effectiveness, in the light of the comparatively small amounts involved, led to international decisions that omitted LNG from IMO Protocols. The non-methane constituents of crude oil include ethane, propane, butane and pentane, and are referred to collectively as NMVOC emissions—or non-methane VOC. The technology for NMVOC recovery is highly complex and works on three principles. The gas is absorbed into the crude oil itself by being soaked up and then liquefied, or condensed and stored in a separate tank. Finally it is adsorbed in carbon filters that hold the gas to the surface of carbon in the filter. The tower observed on boarding housed the condenser and operational controls.

Knutsen OAS Shipping showed the world that it was taking air pollution seriously by using *Anna Knutsen* for initial experiments some years previously, examining how shuttle tankers, which were accused as the biggest offenders, could contribute towards

M/T ANNA KNUTSEN

OFFSHORE LOADING PLAN

OIL FIELD	Statfjord	VOYAGE #	962/06	REMARKS: One deckwatch to be st.by in BLS for at least
LOADING BUOY	OLS-A	CARGO #	SF 6487/2	for 15.min after full rate and VOC is running.
CARGO	Statfjord Crude Oil	QUANTITY	108100 v/15°C	Always keep at least 4 cargo valves open.
DATE	03.08.06	Load. Time	19hrs	Call Chief Officer if any dobt

HRS	1–24
TOT. TIME FOR LOADING	-------→ (to 19)
CT 1	ULLAGE 3,337 M → (to 19)
CT 2	ULLAGE 3,340 M → (to 19)
CT 3	ULLAGE 3,333 M → (to 19)
CT 4	ULLAGE 3,269 M → (to 19)
2A P+S	ULLAGE 2,299 / 4,218 M → (to 17)
2B P+S	ULLAGE 3,069 / 3,089 M → (to 17)
4 P+S	ULLAGE 6,928 / 6,927 M → (to 17)
SLOP P+S	ULLAGE TO BE EMPTY →

CARGO:
COMMENCE LOADING IN ALL WT'S TANKS.
STOP WT4 P/S AT 8,0M ULLAGE, STOP REST OF WT'S ON 6,0M. MONITOR PRESSURE ON BLS MANIFOLD WHILE CLOSING WT'S. CONTINUE ON CT'S
KEEP STERN TRIM ALL THE TIME.
IF NECESSARY USE CARGO TANKS TO MAKE GOOD TRIM FOR THE DEBALLASTING.
USE 2A P/S FOR CORRECTION OF LIST.
CALL CHIEF OFFICER WHEN REMAINING TANKS ARE AT APROX. 7 M ULLAGE.

BALLAST:
Start deballasting as soon as loading has commenced. (Confirm captain).
Draft forward to be kept over 7 meters.
Watch SF and BM, closely
MAX 85% FORCES/ MOMENTS PERMITTED AT SEA CONDITION.
All ballasttanks to be empty before departure,
See attached ballastplan.

DUTY OFFICERS IN BOWHOUSE:
00-06/12-18 : Vestbø/Volden
06-12/18-24 : Santi/Gåssand/Myrvang
WATCHMEN ON DECK:
00-06/12-18 : Kongsro/Bjellerås
06-12/18-24 : Thomassen/Arnevik

DEPARTURE DRAFT:
TF 12,60M
TM 12,65M
TA 12,70M

Test of: Hi. Lev. al. Thruster: X Pumproom P/S: X HPR: X SAAB cleaned: X Bow manif. Greased: X

MASTER: [signature] CH. OFFICER: [signature] JR. CH. OFFICER: [signature]

1ST OFFICER: [signature] 2ND OFFICER: [signature]

Offshore Loading Image for the voyage covering forecasts for all stages of this specific operation including time factors, completion ullages (or free surface area in each tank), and all practical instructions for safe loading (Knutsen OAS).

This was just one of a number of ship checklists whose completion indicated safe performance of any operation directly connected with implementing international and company safety regulations. In many respects, this was the only practical method of ensuring confirmation of each step (Knutsen OAS).

Knutsen OAS Shipping	BRIDGE CHECKLISTS BRIDGE CHECKLISTS SPECIAL SHIP OPERATIONS - SHUTTLE TANKERS	Form no. Rev. no. Originated: Last rev. date: Prep. by: Appr. by Page	VOM07-07 00 30.09.2004 LEH/TL BSE 1 of 1

7.7.0. BRIDGE CHECKLISTS - SPECIAL SHIP OPERATIONS – SHUTTLE TANKERS

Place:	Date/hour:	Voyage no.:

CCRO # 1: DYNAMIC POSITIONING OPERATION:

7.7.1. Approaching Loading Buoy:

Ref	ITEMS	YES	NO	N/A
1	Control of ME, thrusters, rudders and navigation lights transferred from bridge to Bow Control Room (BCR)			
2	Verification that the Position Reference systems (HPR-DGPS-ARTEMIN) have adequate signals, and are working correctly.			
3	Transfer from manual to DP-operation, and verifying Surge, Sway and Yaw.			
4	DP stabilized, and operated for more that 15 minutes.			
5	Verified that "input sensors" for DP-system are working correctly e.g. wind speed, direction etc.			

7.7.2. During Loading:

Ref	ITEMS	YES	NO	N/A
6	Heading- and distance alarm set.			
7	Reference system (PRS) checked.			
8	Alarms and warnings verified.			
9	Distance from loading buoy/base point checked.			

7.7.3. Upon completion of loading / Departure from Loading Buoy:

Ref	ITEMS	YES	NO	N/A
10	"Stand-by Mode" selected on DP prior to departing STL-buoy.			
11	"Stand-by" Mode selected DP and PRS systems.			
12	Main Engine, thrusters, rudders and navigation lights transferred from CBR to Bridge.			

7.7.4. Warning on documentation

Checklist to be completed by Duty Officer, prior to connecting to loading buoy, during loading and after disconnecting from buoy. Verification by making proper entries in Deck Logbook.
Checklist shall be kept "ticked off" until vessel en-route.

7.7.5. Warning

Proper entries in Deck Logbook have to be made prior to arrival/departure/commencement of operation. In case of accidents (collision, grounding etc.), but also in general Port State authorities will not accept missing entries, with Master's intent to make the necessary and obligatory entries in the Logbooks.

Officer of the Watch (Name in print and sign.)

reducing the marine element. The technique devised and adopted by Knutsen Shipping (called KVOC) is unique, because it eliminates the storage tank by stabilising the VOC in the crude oil cargo. The system is technically highly complicated and is achieved partially by loading at a reduced rate, which benefits the environment by cutting up to 90% of emissions and, equally importantly, has proved cost effective. Since its conception,

The Norwegian-owned off-shore tug *Norman Draupne*, purpose-built in 1985, was 3,385 grt with a powerful 18,000 bhp engine and bollard pull of 150 tonnes. This latter calculation, based on complicated formulae, represents the static force on a tow-line exerted continuously by the tug and is the power of the tug to tow an object (Author's Collection).

KVOC has been patented and it is used now by some other operators of shuttle tankers, as well as proving suitable for use with all types of tanker.

At a speed commensurate with maintaining steerage way, *Anna Knutsen* approached the geographic position to pick up the undersea pipeline and commence taking cargo. By this time, the chief officer had completed his loading plan, which had been approved by the Master and signed by all officers, the standard procedures aboard all tankers.

Initial actions during our latter stages of approach were based in the forward superstructure known as the 'bow gatehouse'. It was from here that control and monitoring of both tanker movements and loading were supervised. Engine-room telegraph controls were duplicated and the ship's position was adjusted to keep her on station during any—including the most severe—weather. Such intricate handling was achieved using sophisticated equipment, provided by Kongsberg of Norway, that incorporated a dynamic positioning system using manual controls to manoeuvre the tanker within parameters of accuracy as low as one metre fore and aft. The operation involved in loading relied on settings placed on the loading computer that

The hose from the underwater oil well is gradually lifted aboard *Anna Knutsen* and uncapped before being connected directly to the ship's forward pipe line (Author's Collection).

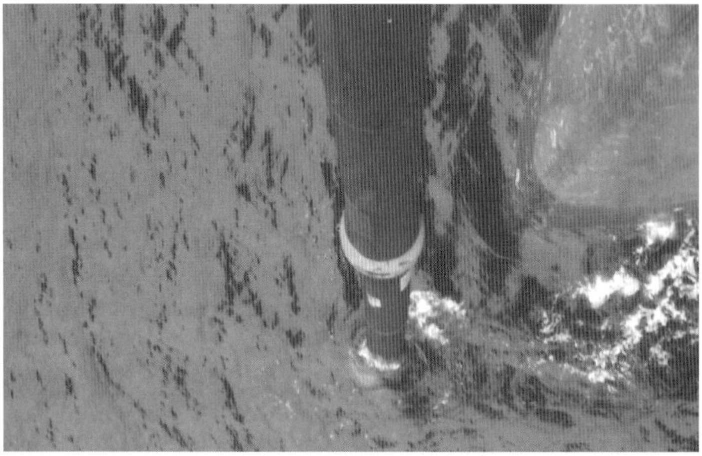

The off-duty Able Seaman spent the time lying quietly to the oil pipe using the hoist by the gangway for fishing, suitably hooked and baited with appetising scraps from the galley, a delightfully human touch that supplemented the excellent fare by a good catch of cod. The hoist was intended officially to bring on board the pilot's bag (Author's Collection).

were closely monitored until cargo completion. The 'green line', the name given to this particular advanced control technology (derived from the colour of the track system on the computer), indicated that essential systems operating this highly complex operation had been set up correctly. Each complex stage was accompanied by rigid adherence to relevant checklists. It was clear that understanding these complicated processes was impossible without intensive background courses ashore.

When the ship was in position, it was closed by a stand by fire-fighting tug and offshore supply vessel that fired a lightweight line that was taken on board and connected through a bow access directly onto a specially provided winch.

Attached to this 'messenger' was a heavier line previously connected to the head of the undersea oil pipe line. Once made fast and slowly winched in, the pipe line was captured by two hydraulic grabs. It was automatically uncapped, and connected to the ship's deck pipe. In the pump room all four cargo-pumps were started and gradually worked to their full capacity of 2880 cu. m/hr. This enabled the crude to be directed along two top and four bottom cargo lines into selected tanks, commencing with the port and starboard Wings, after which oil was directed into the Centre tanks. On this particular voyage, cargo was not pumped into the Slop tanks port and starboard aft, owing to limitations of ship's draught in the River Mersey at Tranmere; thus only 93,923.5 tonnes of cargo, at 113,024.7 cubic metres, were loaded instead of the customary 98% capacity load of 129,154 tonnes. North Sea crude oil is very light, with a specific gravity usually around 0.8321, compared to Arabian heavy crude at 0.8877 or Iranian light at 0.8560.

It was more convenient to transfer loading control during final stages from the gatehouse to the cargo control room. 'Topping-off'—the name given to final stages of tanker loading/discharging aboard conventional tankers—had little significance with shuttle tankers because the process of staggering tank completion in the traditional way was inapplicable to North Sea operations. All Wings were completed by 0509 hours and immediately afterwards loading commenced in the Centre tanks. Lines serving cargo pumps and tanks were interchangeable but because all valves and lines met in Number Four Centre this was the last tank to be loaded. The loading plan had to be modified owing to late running—a common occurrence during any cargo operation—caused on this occasion by differences in the anticipated and actual density of the oil, and the taking of crude at a lower rate than anticipated from a second well. It is impossible to know until arrival the precise specific gravity of the oil to be taken, which inevitably creates some conjecture in the setting of provisional plans. The completion ullages were also affected by essential fuel oil carried in the starboard tanks, leading to a disparity between the final quantity of oil taken in Numbers 2AP and 2AS. Even in the face of these 'hiccups', cargo was completed by 0620, and the Master, chief engineer and relevant officers adjourned again to the bow gate and control centre to let go the underwater pipe. Within five minutes, with the duty officer-of-the-watch in the wheelhouse, *Anna Knutsen* proceeded on passage for her return voyage to Tranmere.

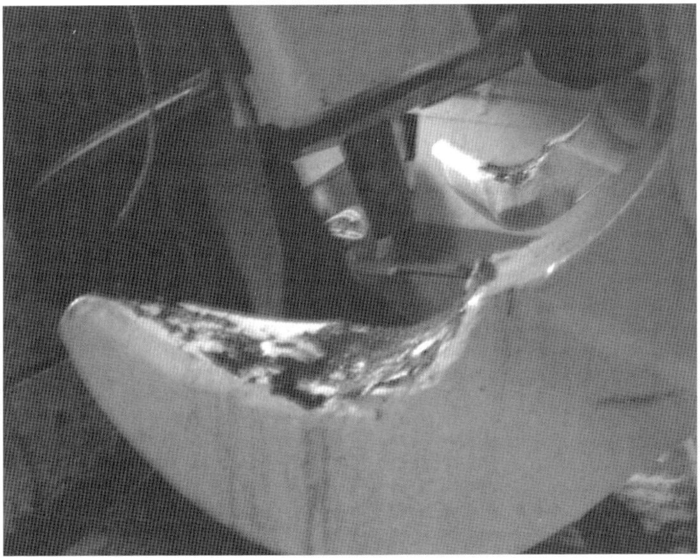

A sideways view of both hydraulic grabs which control the pipeline enabling this to be gently lowered back into the sea and let go from on board the tanker, with nil spillage, a remarkable achievement when compared with the number of tonnes loaded (Author's Collection).

The operation at Statfjord was carried out efficiently, in perfect safety and with due regard to environment, ship and personnel. All crew-members knew what they were doing and quietly got on with it. Flashes of humour, relaxed conversation about spending forthcoming leave—and some mutual teasing—intermingled with intensely serious moments of total concentration. A pleasing ethos existed in the bow gatehouse, created by men carrying out a job in complete continuous control of all stages. The unexpected changes to the Mate's loading plan were dealt with competently and taken in their stride. Initial mild surprise led immediately to planning of compensatory contingency alternatives. These were proposed, provisionally tested, initiated—and then monitored to ascertain efficacy. The atmosphere in the gatehouse was contagious—for even I became immersed in this relaxed ethos and entered into the humour. I asked questions without fear, and grabbed my hard hat with a similar automatic *panache* as any seasoned officer or rating. To do so seemed perfectly natural. There were no histrionics regarding 'what might happen' in terms of potential dangers and unforeseen incidents that could lead to oil spills. I was well aware that the ship was riding differently now that she was well loaded. This knowledge made me regard the vessel in a different light. The tanker was now performing satisfactorily the reason for which she had been constructed. All crew remained well aware of lurking elements of danger, for each knew they were transporting a potentially volatile cargo. A similar attitude would permeate the navigation governing our return passage to the Mersey. A more concentrated air of intensity was subconsciously exhibited by the Master and officers as I watched the navigation of the tanker outward bound to Statfjord in the light of my own experiences. A spill of nearly 100,000 tonnes of crude oil anywhere would have catastrophic effects on the environment—all aboard knew this, but the possibility of this happening *to them* was subjected to making certain it did not.

On this particular voyage, *Anna Knutsen* carried two chief officers and three second mates, conforming to a policy of Knutsen OAS consistent with the appointment of an officer new to shuttle trading. His rank was doubled up for a voyage or two to assist training. In this case, the new officer had been at sea for some years aboard tankers involved on other trades before joining Knutsen OAS. The carrying of a junior chief officer was an additional training practice, for our JCO was an experienced chief and junior officer aboard shuttle tankers who was appointed for extra seagoing experience whilst waiting to join his own ship as senior chief officer.

CHAPTER TWO

Return to Tranmere

During the homeward passage the ship's emergency alarm activated, creating a subtle tenseness in atmosphere as everyone smoothly but determinedly went to their appointed stations. Once I had assimilated within a few seconds what was happening, I joined the orderly passage of crew and reported to the supernumerary's place on the bridge. Here I joined the Master and duty officer whilst, in a controlled atmosphere, investigations into the cause of the alarm were followed, enabling action to be determined, and taken. Subdued tension in the faces of these officers reflected not worry, but intense concentration as thoughts dissected possible situations and dredged for potential remedies in the light of qualifications and experience. I could almost see 'the cogs ticking over' as the competent face of Captain Angell considered ... rejected ... re-considered numerous possibilities, and alternative corrective actions. As it happened, an alarm in the engine-room had fired, for no apparent reason. This had been reset—checked to ascertain correct functioning—and stand-down sounded. The incident was significant for here, happening to me, was a typical example of the fallibility of technology mentioned in my Introduction. This ship—like thousands of others of all classes—could not function without computerisation: and computerisation had proved that it was not without its pitfalls. The Master related an incident that had occurred to him whilst chief officer aboard a crude oil carrier in normal service when a computer fault resulted in failure to record ullages in the cargo control room computer. He was able to supervise cargo and continue loading as normal, largely because of the compulsory IMO-recommended back-up in the form of manual equipment—similar to that with which I had been familiar. It took the chief engineer and electrician four hours to identify the fault, which was due to a card on the master computer that 'had taken a nose-dive'. Two minutes to replace the card, and business proceeded as normal. I shuddered to think of the histrionics certain journalists and reporters would have made of both incidents had they witnessed them. My determination was equally fervent not to fall into a similar trap and write emotionally about 'the millions of gallon aboard' and imagine a range of scenarios, each as likely (or unlikely) as the first, which *might* develop. This was not an occasion for futile imaginations to work overtime.

Following standard practice at sea, the tanker was on automatic pilot for the entire passage once 'Full Away' had been rung on the telegraphs, indicating to the duty engineers that the ship had completed immediate manoeuvres and was on course for the next port. In the event of a 'nautical gremlin' entering the steering system (similar to that in the engine-room earlier) an off-course alarm in the wheelhouse would be activated if the

We passed Fair Isle on the port side keeping to the Traffic Separation Zones in this area designed for safe passage of all shipping by restricting vessels to specific lanes (Author's Collection)

All bridge controls were fully computerised and carefully planned to be within easy access. Here the telegraph controls to both engines are plainly identifiable, as also are the computerised off-course alarm settings to the gyro-controlled automatic steering gear. Usually, the hand wheel was used when a more sensitive and greater control of the steering might be required, invariably when in pilotage waters or sometimes during close-quarter situations with other ships (Author's Collection).

Calm seas and warm temperatures soon heralded dense fog as *Anna Knutsen* passed outside the Outer Hebrides. The ship continued on passage at a safe speed consistent with visibility and traffic conditions, with an extra look-out posted and both radars operational. The Master assessed the situation and advised the officer-of-the-watch to keep him informed of developments and not to hesitate to call him to the wheelhouse as circumstances dictated (Author's Collection).

tanker veered at a predetermined (usually) ten degrees from her course-line—a figure designed to limit the swing of the vessel and avoid embarrassment to passing traffic.

I visited the engine-room whilst we were bound for Tranmere, wearing the customary protective gear and ear defenders. The two main engines were MAN-B&W 9760 bhp operating bronze propellers (comprising 80% copper and 20% nickel). The tanker consumed 49.5 tonnes fuel oil whilst on passage and 35 tonnes during cargo discharge, which included running the Inert Gas System. Nominal amounts of diesel oil operated the ship's incinerator. The vessel had controllable-pitch propellers, 6.1 metres in diameter, with four blades each. The steering gear was made by Kvaerner Prosgrunn and controlled a Becker rudder of rotary vane type operated by pumping oil into one compartment, which reduced oil in an adjacent one. Emphasis on safety and

During every sea passage aboard all ships at sea the deck officer of the watch on duty in the wheel-house keeps active look-out duties for other ships and 'matters of potential navigational significance'; deals with routine telephone calls, keeps an eye on crew working on deck as well as navigating the vessel in coastal waters by placing 'a timed dot on the chart' every thirty minutes. Writing up the log-book at the end of the watch and signing other official documents are also an essential and often legal part of his or her duties (V. Volden).

cleanliness in each area visited, and total concentration by all crew encountered were my lasting impressions. An engineering officer cadet, for example, worked a lathe with such absorbed attention that he was unaware of our presence.

Whilst on passage, the chief officers made an inspection of the tanker's double-bottom area below the water ballast tanks

Ships' engineering officers are invariably a cheerful yet highly responsible bunch and are seen here at the main engine and auxiliary controls panel (V. Volden).

The main engine of a typical shuttle tanker showing the seven cylinder heads (V. Volden).

on the starboard side aft. This was a routine check designed to allow inspection of all double-bottom ballast tanks over a series of mini-voyages. The general condition of the plating, evidence of pitting, cracking, and 'anything out of the ordinary that might meet the eye' determined the criteria for examination. Most non-dry-dock inspections had to be cursory because surface areas were vast, lit only by powerful torches and in comparatively difficult spaces in which to lumber around. Access to Number 5SWB tank was by a watertight bolted circular hole in the main deck just by the VOC tower. When we arrived after morning 'smoke-oh', the bosun had erected safety railings around the access hole, so the three of us climbed down onto the ladder leading to the bottom of the tank. The bosun or apprentice-AB stood by at the top of the tank and remained in vhf communication continuously whilst our party was below. Once at the bottom, we climbed through further rat-holes in the deck to the double bottom-tank.

The two and half metre depth made standing upright comfortable and helped our well-being. It also assisted the

The ladders leading from the main deck access hole to the bottom of the ballast tank, and then into the double bottom. These spaces generally contain ballast water when the tanker has discharged cargo and is on passage for further loading. The ladders are perfectly safe to use, but those leading to the double bottom can feel cramped in the necessary safety and protective gear (Author's Collection).

inspection. There were few surprises on reaching the tank bottom and it was as I expected: dark, dank from the ballast water that had been discharged during loading at Statfjord, and quite stuffy in our full deck gear complete with hard hat and boots. It was not consistently easy to clamber through the inspection rat-holes in the deck plating, and mouse-holes cut into the verticals of the longitudinal and transversal plating making up the cellular construction of the tank. It was warm, and caution was required at all stages whilst treading through slippery mud (and small dead fish) accumulated on the tank bottom from Mersey ballast water. The junior chief officer went off alone to inspect the after part of the tank, whilst I accompanied the Mate to look forward. Whilst wandering the maze of tank sections we discussed current IMO proposals currently receiving legislation for environmental protection regarding the transference of ballast water from one part of the world to another, with likely pollution implications. The condition of the tanks was excellent considering the age of the ship. There was no evidence of cracking—a thing for which we looked in particular—and very little pitting or plate corrosion. Tank coatings remained effective and seemed as good as when they had been applied. The only striking note was slight signs of corrosion at some tank corners, but scraping revealed this was only superficial and had not penetrated into the plate. Owing to its slow advance it could best be left untreated, but noted for the attention of future chief officers. The inspection was thorough—within the parameters available—and time consuming, following which we clambered up the ladders into fresh air and lunch. In the afternoon, an inspection of the ballast tank itself occurred, for as good a look as was feasible. Our powerful torches cast subdued light into tank corners, looking for evidence of cracking or plate corrosion or shifting, especially at tank corners and across the tank top.

Following IMO codes, Knutsen OAS instituted a systematic policy aboard ships encouraging reporting of 'near misses'

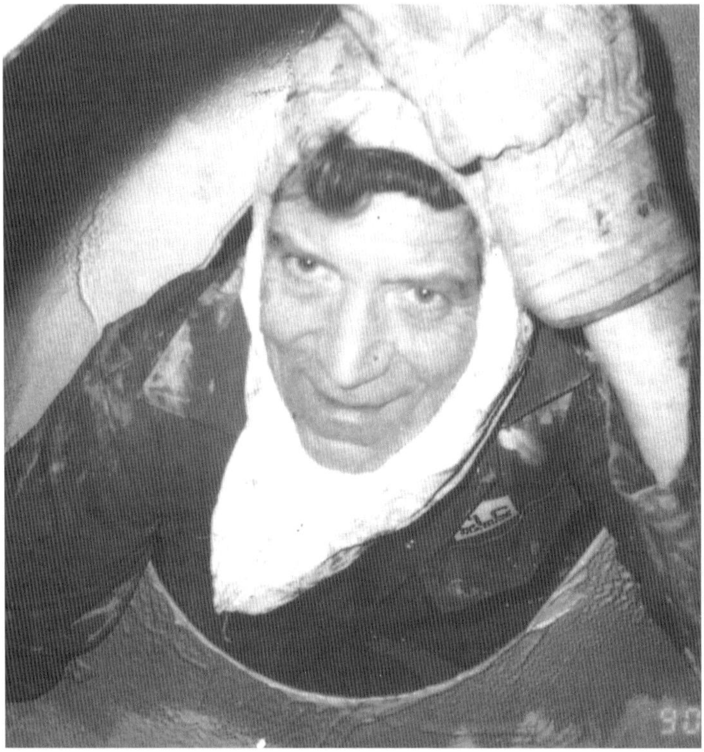

Entering the tank was always an exercise in agility, but such inspections were essential to detect as practically as possible any visible defects which might have occurred since the previous inspection. With tanks aboard the larger ships that could easily accommodate a small cathedral, the task was difficult and 100% efficiency could not be expected. An overall impression, combined with years of experience concerning what 'good' and 'bad' tanks look like, made possible a useful practical assessment regarding the state of any tank. This is about the best that could be expected or achieved (Jotun Paints, Europe, Ltd and Victor Pyrate Ltd).

which, in the words of a Company manual, 'cover events that have potential of causing damage to life, health, vessels, material or environment'. A film taken on board the *Anneleen Knutsen* accompanied the brochure showing everyday jobs of the type encountered specifically on shuttle tankers. The film was of value to the wider industry as many of the incidents covered proved typical of those met aboard most seagoing tankers. The film commenced '...with everything going amiss. The jobs are not planned well enough, nor has any safety assessment of the tasks to be done been carried out. On top of it all, the second sequence shows examples of other things that could have gone wrong as a result of the way the jobs are done'. In the final part,

Knutsen OAS Shipping

KNUTSEN OAS SHIPPING AS
Smedasundet 40
P.O. Box 2017
N-5504 HAUGESUND

Tel.: (47) 52 70 40 00
Fax: (47) 52 70 40 40
Telex: 42 204 KNUT

NO 832 529 982 MVA

NEAR MISS REPORT FORM

This form should be used to report to near miss incidents so they can be discussed and action taken to prevent a possible accident.

Please do not enter names or ranks as the only intent of this form is to assist in preventing future accidents - not to attribute blame to individuals.

Type of Near Miss

- ☐ Incorrect or Misuse of Equipment and Systems
- ☐ Incorrect, Misuse or Lack of, PPE
- ☐ Incorrect or Misuse of Tools
- ☐ Working without Permits or Procedures
- ☐ Almost Slip or Fall, (or very minor)
- ☐ Almost Struck-by
- ☐ Almost Cut By
- ☐ Housekeeping
- ☐ Other please state: ....

Location of Near Miss: ....

Time of Near Miss: ....

Description: ....

'Near Miss Report Form', which all crew-members are encouraged to complete and hand-in to the Master through their head of department whenever they are involved in any kind of mishap that might have led to an accident–however slight this may have been. This information is then discussed by senior officers and recommendations made as necessary to the Captain, that are passed to the respective head office department for action, as well as being discussed in detail on board ship (Knutsen OAS).

the same work receives a re-examination, but shown this time as practised 'according to the book'. The company distributed aboard their ships report forms to be completed whenever a near miss occurs in any department on board.

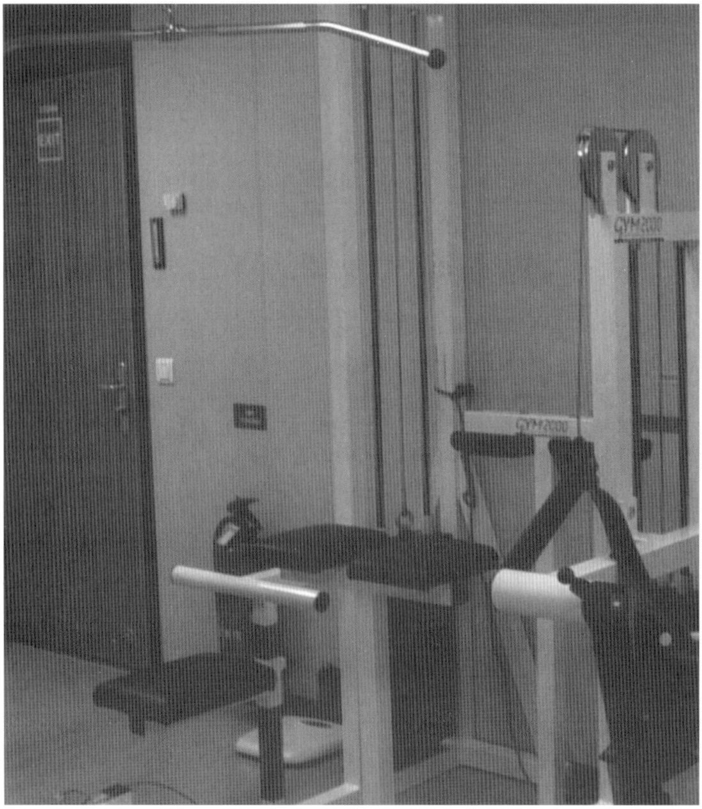

Opportunity was taken on the homeward passage to use the ship's washing machines for personal laundry, drying this afterwards in the hot facility provided and giving shirts a treat by running them over with the ship's iron. A few welcome but not too exacting sessions were also spent in the quiet of the evening in the well equipped gymnasium (V. Volden).

Our passage to the Mersey gave me ample opportunity for reflection. There were fewer crew-members on board than expected, which meant limited time for deck maintenance duties although, as it has been shown, many of these were carried out. For six months the ship carried a Polish painting party. When their deck duties were affected by inclement weather they worked in board painting store-rooms, or on routine maintenance. There was little socialising compared to yesteryear, especially in a 'dry' officers' smoke-room bar and, apart from visits to the communal lounge for television or video games—or to the gymnasium for a workout—whole evenings could be spent solitary in the lounge, flicking through magazines or watching videos or television. Different pursuits had replaced traditional cards, chess, or social drinking, doubtless reflecting cultural changes in life ashore. Fewer crew-members meant more men resting in preparation for watches. Life aboard tankers today may well be far safer than in my time, but it offers too many opportunities for introspection. In keeping with many others, I spent most spare time in the cabin, in my case reading masses of official paperwork and planning activities for the next day. Wandering around alleyways at various moments during day and evening was akin to being aboard the *Mary Celeste*. There was little sign of life. After just a couple of days, life at sea aboard tankers of this class and trade had little appeal—especially for a trip of any length.

There existed a further downside. I was appalled at the amount of paperwork encountered, much of which was difficult for seafarers to comprehend without attending shore courses. This was a two-edged sword, for these same regulations, rules, protocols and their accompanying mass of paperwork represented the very lifeblood of the safety procedures I was being privileged to witness.

My opportunity to clarify puzzling issues came after we cleared the Scottish coast on the run into the Irish Sea when, with his discharging plan completed, I sat down with the senior chief officer summarising my observations aboard *Anna Knutsen*. A first concern centred upon officers' ability to cope with endless paperwork and how they kept abreast and understood this. The answer implied that all officers (as I had observed) follow legislation, although 'a certain kind of madness exist[ed]' in the amount they had to digest. The secret, to the chief officer, seemed to lie in having thorough knowledge of most legislation, accompanied by an ability 'to find your way around the Regs, knowing where to look, so that when you wish to check something, you know where it will be found.' We discussed backgrounds of the United Nations Convention on the Law of the Sea (UNCLOS), created in 1982 to work within the auspices of the International Maritime Organization (IMO), and International Labour Organization (ILO). Both aimed to establish rules governing responsibilities of flag-owning States towards the safety of the environment from pollution; the training and safety of seafarers, and other legislative commitments. For the mariner, IMO regulations presented the framework of safety, training and pollution prevention, whilst ILO concerns remained with working and living conditions at sea. The SOLAS Convention mentioned provided for International Management Codes for Safe Operation of Ships and Pollution Prevention—known as the ISM Code, which was instituted in 1995 to work with established MARPOL, STCW, load-line and tonnage regulations. Ship owners responsible for managing and operating any specific ship work in partnership with their vessel by implementing a Shipboard Management Safety System (SMS). Designated persons both in the Company offices ashore and aboard are responsible through the Master for performing audits designed to review regularly the procedures for safety on board ship. As a direct result of the *Erika* and *Prestige* disasters, the major oil companies organisation OCIMF (Oil Companies International Marine Forum) introduced the Tanker

Management Self Assessment Scheme (TMSA) which has had an instrumental effect on the industry both ashore and afloat.

It seemed there were no 'quick fixes', for it remains impossible to risk assess every single event likely to happen, in the same way that it is impossible to legislate for any event occurring in life. We live in a world where virtually all things have an ability to go 'pear-shaped', because all things have a difficult, or impossible to assess, built-in risk. The various ship management codes offer eminently practical advice to conundrums that might happen at sea, declaring an unequivocally correct and accident-free way of performing jobs. Directly an out-of-the-norm incident is encountered anywhere on board—in engine-room, on the bridge, down a tank, or in the accommodation—reporting this to another person becomes essential, by telephone or by sounding an emergency alarm. Such action shares the problem, creates awareness of an abnormality, and provides the Master—and others—with sufficient time to plan actions, and to put these into effect. Such incidents can then be dealt with summarily, or followed up using 'near miss' reporting. These then become subjects of discussion and investigation during one of the daily shipboard meetings at 1300 hours, and notified as necessary to the management designated-person ashore. Remedial action may result with either a checklist, or one of many safety signs adorning backs of doors, alleyway bulkheads or cabins.

It was to comply with such shipboard codes that shipboard safety committees were established. Their purpose was to meet regularly and discuss incidents or hazardous situations which may have happened on board, enquire how these hazards were discovered, and propose remedial action. It was implementation of these codes that encouraged crew-members to act in a team by following procedures and completing checklists, within the parameters of each person's own duty. Careful planning ensured shipboard jobs became assessed for potential risk with a job description analysis confirming the work of each seafarer. This created individual awareness of tasks and ensured everyone on board was aware of the work of others so that a practical scheme of mutual support became fostered. The ethos of the management system encouraged moves away from rigidity. It provided a flexible structure permitting amendments where necessary as circumstances changed or 'an improved way of doing things' became apparent—or, even better, as new hazards were identified. Checklists provided practical summaries of legislation and, from the point of view of many (but not all) became 'worth their weight in gold' to busy seafarers doing the job practically. They *helped* reduce human errors of omission or commission—or even 'short-circuiting' the system, to which we are all prone—and encouraged mutual confidence among crew. Potential downsides to completing checklists might be suggestions that 'this' method is the only one doing the job, and that familiarity could breed contempt resulting in a 'rote approach'. The remedy for these negatives was foreseen in this well thought through package by suggesting comprehensive courses ashore, in-board training sessions, and senior and junior officer supervision. Such regulatory measures helped seafarers gain better understanding of why each task had to be done. The Company also provides shipboard safety-management manuals covering key shipboard operations, including a regular maintenance programme with designated areas covering future areas for planning.

Other examples of responsible management place emphasis on ensuring familiarity of personnel with equipment germane to their job. This is done by training and duplicating key personnel for short voyages. The idea of 'getting to know what things do' was encouraged and practised—both for safety and efficiency, and to lessen strain on the Master and senior officers. Regular training seminars held ashore for all officers and ratings included rafts of multi-level company-sponsored courses for senior and junior officers and ratings, covering basic safety, tanker certification, various highly specialist items of equipment (such as tanker safety endorsement courses, dynamic positioning and VOC), and ship management. Senior personnel acknowledged their accountability to their crew by setting examples in wearing correct gear for all occasions and not becoming 'slapdash' in this. It meant visitors to the ship were also expected to conform to similar established standards—witnessed by the crew—all contributing to safety becoming a realistic way of life. Listening to *Anna Knutsen*'s experienced chief officer explaining these circumstances reinforced in my mind the importance of such regulations—and the need for their implementation.

It was nevertheless impossible for me to consider much that I had heard without casting my mind back to the reception afforded these ideas in my own seafaring days. I asked the chief officer 'Is this Code seen as just another piece of paper?' —'Can this be useful?'—'If I complete a "near miss" form, will it be taken seriously by head office?' It seemed appropriate to enquire what levels of support were offered *practically* by the Company. Admittedly, whilst acting as devil's advocate, I offered a red herring by suggesting that 'so long as something fulfilled legal requirements, could there be concern for implementing possible improvements to it?' I took the safety-cum-working boat (not the lifeboat) as my randomly selected example that whilst 'it might fulfil legal requirements, it might not be found up to its job, perhaps lacking sufficient power for its engine, so would it just sit ignored on its chocks?' We exchanged a wry smile as I presented this to the Mate who responded by saying that upon discovery, head office would be notified of the under-performance with a request for fitting a more powerful engine—and this would happen. I enquired how such an approach might be made to head office other than, say, by the 'near miss' system and discovered the opportunity for doing so could be brought about at an end-of-voyage conference. He quoted how a recent interface at head office received 296 suggestions for improvements from seagoing personnel and asked me, in turn, to guess how many had been implemented. I thought a little and gave a figure which to my mind sounded reasonable in the light of my own experience of 'interfacing' (not that we called it that) with head office during my own sea days. He retorted by informing me that 275 had been discussed positively and *virtually all implemented* without further delay or question. Of the 21 not considered viable, most saw referral for additional enquiry or examination. Even a number of the ubiquitous checklists received scrutiny, and some were revised as a result. It seemed the situation regarding paperwork confronting today's seafarers was not going to change. It was here to stay, had to be accepted as a fact of maritime life, and followed—considering that reassuring assistance existed to help mariners cope positively without excessive overburdening.

For the most part, the international shipping industry has taken TMSA/ISM/SMS codes seriously; senior seafarers have been appointed by flag-state operators as Audit Inspectors with mandatory rights to visit any ship and speak to any seafarer, enquiring to what extent the codes might be implemented aboard their ship. Well-founded and run ships have little to fear once their reputation has become established and are likely to experience fewer visits when revisiting any specific port. The powers of port inspectors are paramount, for visited ships which fail to implement the codes can be prevented from sailing until any failure is rectified.

The conversations not only with the Mate but with the Master and other officers still left unanswered questions and I soon realised that I would have to look elsewhere for satisfaction—probably to authoritative organisations ashore. I wrote myself a personal memorandum.

We approached Lynas Point pilot station early on the ninth day of my trip, a few hours before the time forecast on our Voyage Waypoint Plan, owing to speed increases arising from favourable tidal streams. The tanker moved easily in a calm sea with low swell and a light westerly wind wafting around Force One or Two. We coasted slowly off the Point awaiting correct tidal conditions for berthing at Tranmere. It was not worth using either of the two 14-tonne anchors, because the time to drop one of these (in such ideal weather conditions) and then weigh it would not have been justified. The two pilots boarded at 1630 hours and the vessel was put to the time-honoured logbook abbreviation, VTMOPA, or: 'Vessel to Master's Orders

Taking the pilot aboard from his cutter was an operation familiar to most ships manoeuvring in confined waters where the carriage of this ex-ship's master trained in local knowledge of tides, currents, shipping density and weigh-points, was mandatory. The pilot was always taken according to clearly defined and strict regulations for boarding was not always in the excellent weather conditions portrayed here, but frequently took place in rough seas and strong winds. During these occasions, the ship would swing and make a lee, offering at least a measure of calm water during boarding and dropping the pilot (Author's Collection).

An active scene in the wheelhouse as *Anna Knutsen* proceeds on passage from Lynas Point towards her berth at Tranmere. The experimental computerised chart system is clearly visible showing the ship's track (Author's Collection).

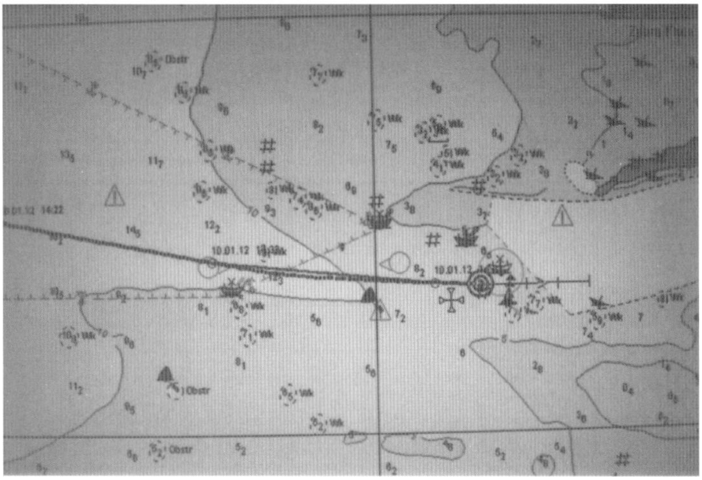

A close-up shot of the computerised chart indicating approaches to the River Mersey. The Bar Light vessel is shown slightly to the north of the centre of the photograph, whilst the Formby light float may be seen to the right. The differing shades (which are blue on screen) indicate depths of water within the ten, five and one metre bands (Author's Collection).

and Pilots' Advice'. It was mandatory for all tankers entering Liverpool waters within the tonnage of the *Anna Knutsen* to carry two pilots, who were in constant communication with Liverpool VTS, the Vessel Tracking Service—operated by the port control harbour-master and his staff that regulated all ship movements within the Mersey and approach waters.

It was 2000 hours before we took the tug *Eskgarth* in attendance (but not made fast) aft, and eight minutes later we entered the buoyed channel, proceeding at a speed of 4.8 knots commensurate with safety in the existing conditions of tides and traffic. The vessel proceeded at a reduced speed of 10.8 knots, in heavy rainsqualls and reduced visibility, for the 30-odd-mile passage, past the Bar and Formby Light floats to the buoyed channel into the River Mersey. Pilots never take chances, and their approach to a minor tidal rip as we entered the buoyed channel was handled with professional decisiveness and calm. Tongue in cheek, I broached the question concerning occasions when a Master might overrule the advice of his pilot, citing an incident I had witnessed in the Arabian Gulf as a second officer on bridge-watch during the berthing of a Very Large Crude Carrier (VLCC). The Captain considered the pilot had approached the jetty at too critical an angle and requested him to abort the operation, 'take a round turn' and reapproach. I mentioned the pilot's chagrin but told how, seeing a certain glint in the Master's eye, he did as asked—albeit with some bad grace. Thus prompted, both of our pilots drew on their foreign-going and coastal experiences. It was agreed within collective reflections that such incidents had never occurred in any north-European port, but instances were quoted when pilots had indeed been overruled. A striking occasion occurred during a berthing at Dar-es-Salaam when the Master considered the pilot aboard a 10,000 grt dry-cargo ship was approaching the berth too quickly commensurate with existing circumstances and conditions. He advised a speed reduction about which the pilot argued. The Master acted by moving the telegraph lever and slowing the ship, so preventing collision with a closing Arabian dhow. The pilot later agreed the Master's action had been correct. The discussion proved quite an interesting talking-point as we gently rounded the fairway buoys leading to Liverpool.

A second tug, *Ashgarth*, joined us at 2125 hours and as we approached the berth both tugs were made fast fore and aft.

The tanker was in position with manifolds, Chiksans and gangway connections lined up, and the vessel put her first line ashore, a forward breast rope, and was made fast, with tugs

Taking the tug aft requires her to come under the stern of own vessel and take the tug's wire usually to cover insurance purposes which is placed according to the requirements of the senior pilot (V. Volden).

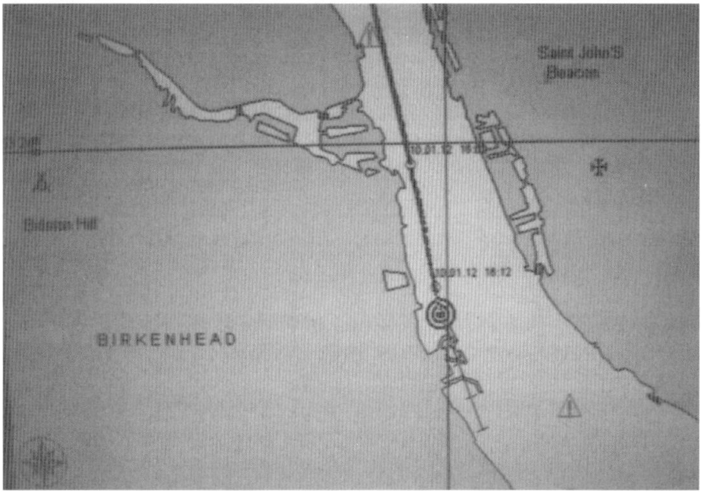

Our approach to the berth showed clearly on the chart system and the rate of approach may be deduced from observation of the ten-minute time positions indicated. The system had lived up to expectations throughout the time of its use on the voyage and had proved reliable and accurate (Author's Collection).

and pilots away, at 2240 hours. The berthing operation had taken almost one-and-a-half hours from the time we took the second tug. Following a visit from shore inspectors and with appropriate regulatory officials negotiating with the Master and chief officer, cargo discharge commenced just after midnight.

A washing programme extending over a range of voyages had been planned using alternate tanks, with Number Three Centre and Two Wing tanks selected upon completion of the Tranmere discharge. Two pumps were fitted for crude oil washing, each of 1000 cubic metres per hour. A number of tank-cleaning machines were fitted to the top and bottom of each tank, each with a single nozzle directing a powerful jet of concentrated ship's cargo at the tank bottom and sides to remove as much of the oil as possible. In view of the construction of Wing tanks, some shadow areas existed, but modern machines meant these represented just a tiny percentage. Centre tank cleaning took twenty minutes for the top wash and forty for the bottom, with the smaller Wing tanks taking thirty minutes and twenty respectively.

I remained on board covering the various stages of discharging the crude oil, based mainly in the cargo control room where I had focussed immediately upon joining the tanker ten days previously.

My thoughts crystallised and were far from nostalgic as I crossed the gangway at 1500 hours the following day after witnessing parts of the ballasting and tank-washing operations prior to leaving *Anna Knutsen*. My time aboard had lived up to expectations perfectly. I should have liked to remain longer, but felt ready to begin additional research in earnest. It was quite surprising to find little hankering for 'the good old days', probably because, as the novelist L.P. Hartley succinctly stated: 'The past is a foreign country: they do things differently there.' On my trip I had witnessed many changes since my own seafaring, most of which were positive. There were no incidents of drunken seafarers or any under the influence of drugs. There are fewer accidents to personnel. *Anna Knutsen* had a computerised board, which on my last day indicated that there had been 1780 totally accident-free days—equivalent to nearly *five years* of overall safety. This figure included minor accidents or incidents as well as major occurrences and has resulted from greater awareness that the potential for incidents is always present and that these can happen. It

The discharge and crude oil washing plan, showing ballasting operations forecast and appropriate times for these to commence. If everything went according to the plan, cargo would have been discharged in just under sixteen hours, indicating that pilots and tugs would have been booked provisionally for twenty-four hours after arrival (Knutsen OAS).

Discharge / Cow Plan M/T Anna Knutsen

Port: Arrival Tranmere ☑ Discharging ☐ Loading Date 31.07.06

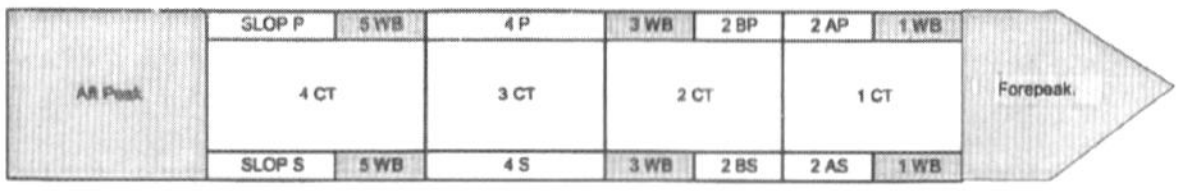

PORT: Arrival Tranmere
VOY: 961/06
GRADE: Statfjord Crude Oil
CARGO NO. SF 6484/2

GRADE	TONNES	PORT	QUANTITY M3
Statfjord Crude Oil	93923.5	Arrival Tranmere	113024.7
Arrival Draft :	Fwd 12.80 Mtr	Aft 13.00 Mtr	

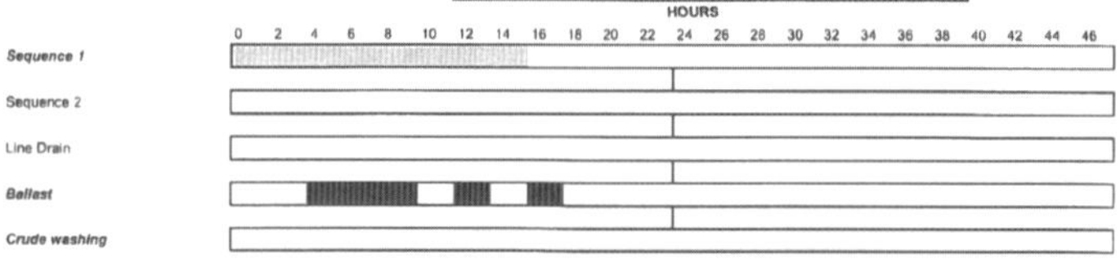

	Before Discharge					Discharge			Complete Discharge		Destination
Tank	Ullage	Cub. Mtr.	Met.Tonnes	Density	Temp	Pump	No of Bottom Line	No. Of Top Line	Final Ullage	Quantity Remaining	
2AP	2.01	3260.2	2684.3	0.8321	25.3°	All if need	4	2	20.76	0	Arrival Tranmere
2BP	3.07	3332.1	2744.6	0.8321	24.9°	All if need	4	2	20.75	0	Arrival Tranmere
4P	3.52	5833.4	4806.3	0.8321	24.6°	All if need	4	2	20.74	0	Arrival Tranmere
SLP	17.35	0.0	0.0	0.8321	25.0°	All if need	4	2	17.35	0	Arrival Tranmere
CT1	2.80	21101.4	17324.8	0.8321	28.5°	All if need	4	2	21.7	0	Arrival Tranmere
CT2	2.75	23051.6	18929.9	0.8321	28.3°	All if need	4	2	21.7	0	Arrival Tranmere
CT3	2.87	22902.6	18815.1	0.8321	27.8°	All if need	4	2	21.7	0	Arrival Tranmere
CT4	2.79	22779.7	18700.9	0.8321	28.6°	All if need	4	2	21.7	0	Arrival Tranmere
2AS	4.28	2857.6	2352.8	0.8321	25.3°	All if need	4	2	20.75	0	Arrival Tranmere
2BS	3.06	3337.8	2750.2	0.8321	24.6°	All if need	4	2	20.77	0	Arrival Tranmere
4S	3.52	5843.0	4814.7	0.8321	24.5°	All if need	4	2	20.74	0	Arrival Tranmere
SLS	17.35	0.0	0.0	0.8321	23.9°	All if need	4	2	17.32	0	Arrival Tranmere
TOTAL		114299.2	93923.5	Average	27.6°						

ADDITIONAL INSTRUCTIONS: **LINEDISPLACEMENT SEE BOARD FOR MORE INFORMATION**
CHECK THAT FIXED GAS SYSTEM FOR PUMPROOM IS WORKING. IF IG-SYSTEM STOPS, STOP DISCHARGING.
RESUME DISCHARGING FROM CT'S, THEN ALSO ON WT'S
USE CP 2, 3 & 4. THE OFFICER ON WATCH SHOULD CHECK THE PRESSURES OF PV VALVES UPON
RECEIVING WARNING SIGNAL/ALARM AND SHALL REDUCE OR STOP THE CARGO TRANSFER OF THE TANK AND INFORM THE CHIEF OFFICER IMMIDIATELY.
BE AWARE OF H2S CONTENT IN THE CARGO. CALL CHIEF OFFICER AND DUTY ENGINEER IF I.G. PROBLEMS OCCURS.
SHEARFORCES AND BENDING MOMENT TO BE OBSERVED CAREFULLY DURING THE WHOLE OPERATION.
CALL CHIEF OFFICER WHEN 1M SOUNDING ON 2AP/S.
COW TO BE CARRIED OUT IN WT2AP/S AND CT 3.
BALLAST / DEBALLAST INSTRUCTIONS
BALLASTING TO BE CARRIED OUT ACCORDING TO BALLAST PLAN. TRY TO FILL IN WHEN SLACK WATER. USE WB1DB1 P/S FOR LIST.
DEPARTURE DRAUGHT APROX.: TF 8.50 m. TA 8.50 m.

BUNKERING INSTRUCTIONS

SIGNED CHIEF ENGINEER

PERSONELL INVOLVED IN CARGO OPERATION:

	DUTY OFFICER	DECKWATCH
0000 - 0400 / 1200 - 1600	Vestbø	Thommasen / Bjelterås
0400 0800 / 1600 2000	Volden	Split
0800 1200 / 2000 2400	Santi	Arnevik / Kongsro

DUTIES: DUTY OFFICER TO PROGRESS THE OPERATIONS OUTLINED ABOVE. UNDER THE DIRECTIONS OF THE CHIEF OFFICER

DECKWATCH TO ASSIST WITH CARGO OPERATION, MOORING AND GANGWAY AS REQUIRED (SEE OWN CHECKLIST)

CHIEF OFFICER [signature]
CHIEF OFFICER JR [signature]
1 ST OFFICER [signature]
APPROVED BY MASTER [signature]
2 ND OFFICER [signature]

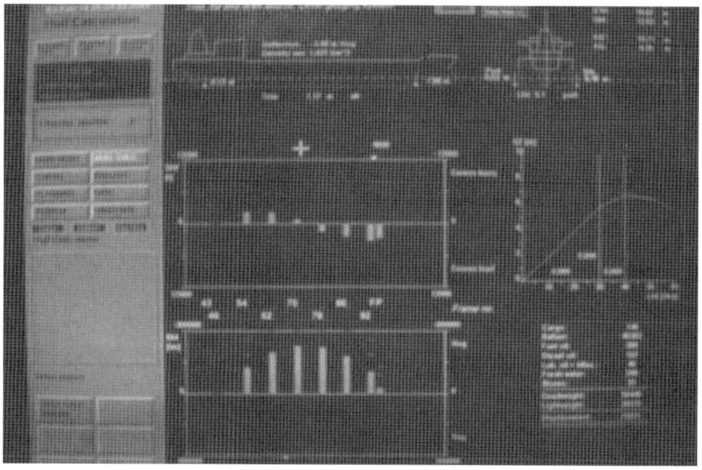

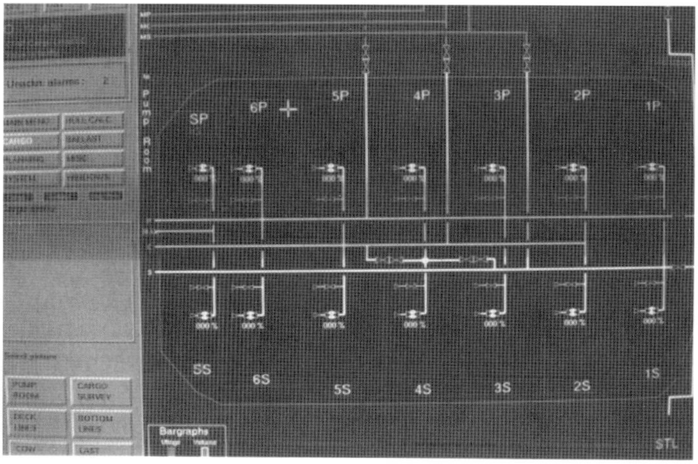

Cargo control during all loading and discharging operations is a time of deep concentration on computer screens analysing the information gleaned and keeping in direct contact with those on deck and in the engine-room. There are many different aspects of the deck officer's work that he has to keep constantly in mind, such as hull stresses in terms of shearing forces and bending moments, and the situations regarding operation of the bottom tank lines and pump room controls. The list is virtually endless but requires an awareness of all that is going on associated with the operation concerned even during those many occasions when things seem to be going well and a momentary relaxing may be permitted (V. Volden).

has meant that a greater number of seafarers have become proactive and increasingly on their guard for conditions leading to dangerous situations involving themselves, their colleagues, the environment—and reassuringly, their ship. Even as a mere visitor I was more aware of safety than I had been aboard any previous tanker upon which I had served operationally. No damage was caused from oil spills to the environment where this vessel sailed, the seas remained cleaner as garbage was incinerated or placed ashore rather than thoughtlessly ditched over the side. There was limited air pollution. I was mindful of many gaps in my own knowledge in understanding the technical side of the cargo and berthing operations observed, especially concerning some of the newer computerised equipment, and recognised the importance of shore-side courses to serving crew, helping them gain theoretical insight before practising this operationally.

My trip on *Anna Knutsen* proved that safety is currently a major concern to seafarers, shipowners and supporting agencies, and rightly so. The days when major oil spills were shrugged off with little responsibility—and an occasional apology have (thankfully) receded into the past. This is due directly to the rigorous attention paid to every aspect of safety aboard tankers. I looked forward with interest to examining recent historical background with a view to finding out how this impressive regard for regulations came into existence—because transporting crude oil at sea in the past has certainly lacked such strict attention. Relaxing in the taxi, I was convinced the 'man in the street' could be reliably informed and reassured that the petrol in his car and the vast array of refined products are carried by responsible personnel who remained conscientious over doing their respective jobs.

CHAPTER THREE

Around the Skagerrak

A courtesy car met me at Schipol Airport and, following a visit to the police and immigration for clearance to join BP Shipping's *British Ensign*, I encountered again the rigid security of an oil terminal. Driving to the berth, I caught the pungent smells of excess gases being burnt and noticed how the harsh electric lighting produced stark outlines from tank farms, piping and processing equipment. Emphasised against a dark starry night sky at 0200 hours, the sight was bizarre and rather eerie. Of more significance, as a direct result of my research, the vaguely 'romantic' atmosphere I had previously associated with refineries was displaced by focussed awareness of air pollution, at a time when the tankers serving these same farms were rigidly regulated to assist elimination of similar effects.

The customary warm welcome followed my arrival on board and I met the officer-of-the-watch in the cargo control room where he was experiencing a brief delay in cargo discharge due euphemistically to 'shore problems'. A cup of tea and a nibble from a plate of covered sandwiches left available for me, and then it was off to the Owner's Cabin (the perennial accommodation berth aboard most tankers for transient visitors),

BP Shipping's *British Ensign* is a crude oil/products carrier of 36,713 s-dwt, on a summer draught of 11.316 metres, giving a freeboard of 5.913 m. She is 184.22 m length overall (176 m bp) x 27.4 extreme beam x 17.2 m moulded depth. From the top of the funnel to the keel is 45.51 metres. Hyundai Mipo Dock in Ulsan, South Korea built the tanker. Her keel was laid on 5th December 2005 and the tanker delivered to the owners and leased to BP Shipping Limited, 26th April 2006. Additional to the now compulsory double-hull, the ship was specially strengthened under Ice Classification Regulations for service in Baltic and Scandinavian waters. In October, the tanker was seven months into service, during which time she had performed with encouraging results and few problems (BP Shipping and Ken Smith).

a quick unpacking of gear and under the duvet for a restful night's sleep. The availability of a spare cabin is invaluable for supernumerary travellers, including company superintendents and inspectors carried for official inspection audits required by flag-state authorities. The cabin was comfortably furnished and equipped and I was well looked after by an Indian mess-man who, it transpired, would have an uncanny, but delightfully acceptable knack of appearing at numerous moments offering cups of tea and, during the late afternoon, a welcome mug of soup. It was delightful to be back with Asian crew and to see how naturally and professionally they undertook their duties. As much writing of my research was by laptop and memory stick, these interruptions were readily accepted.

At breakfast next morning I met the Indian Master and Chief Engineer, quickly establishing a strong rapport especially when relating how in the melee of leaving home, arranging air flights, transport to Stansted Airport, and hastily packing—I had left behind my changes of shirts and trousers. My wife had mentioned when I phoned her at the airport something about 'clothes on the wardrobe door' but, in the impetus of the moment,

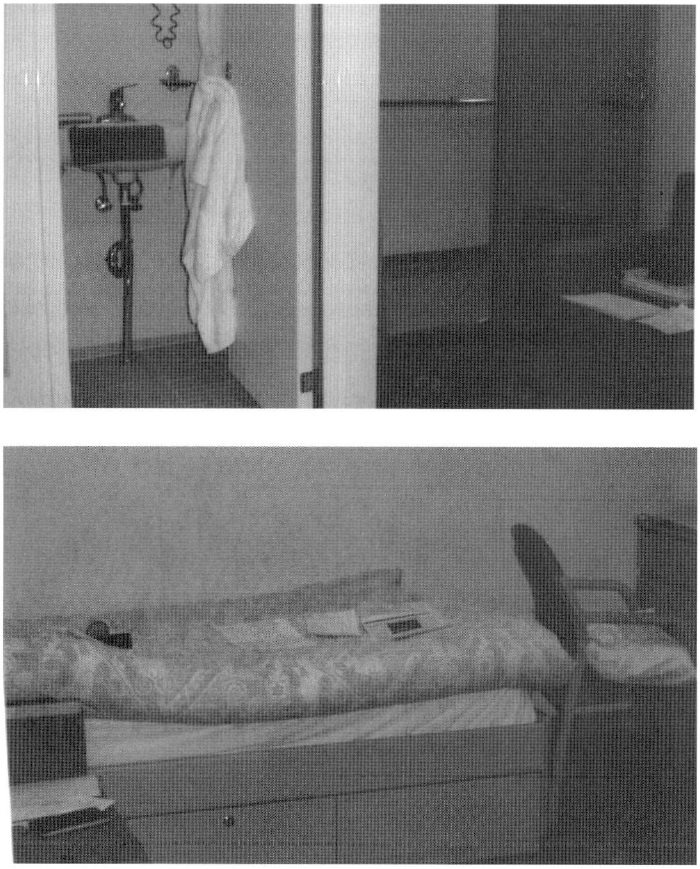

The well-equipped and comfortable Owner's Cabin was fully en-suite and looked after by a very attentive messman. This cabin was occasionally used by visiting company superintendents and sundry other officials invariably engaged on following performance audits, as well as a very rare itinerant author (Author's Collection).

her comment did not immediately register. It was only after showering on board and looking for clean gear that I realised—with an accompanying tremor of horror—the enormity of my 'clanger'. As an icebreaker, however, I could have introduced no better topic, and the conversation went along the following lines as the three of us tucked into our meal:

'How is the merchant naval sense of humour aboard this ship, Captain?'

'Fine—so far as I know.' A querulous glance across the table to the Chief as they both clearly wondered what might be coming next.

'Ah, that's encouraging because you see, I have left at home half of my gear and, apart from full sets of underclothes and the like, have only the trousers and shirt in which I travelled earlier this morning.'

Gales of laughter followed this sally in which I found myself joining (more ruefully) as suggestions concerning what might be done zoomed between the three of us. Ideas covered a range of fancies including my sailing the voyage in a boiler suit. The Master then appeased my fears, explaining how our delay on this berth meant we had lost our place on the next berth and—like stacked dominoes collapsing—would not be leaving the following day as anticipated. Consequently, a visit had been arranged to the nearby Botlek Stores for a shopping spree; there was plenty of room for me in the minibus to accompany this foraging expedition. My sigh of relief was almost audible. It seemed his teasing proved indeed the continued efficacy of shipboard fun. With this problem solved, it was down to ship's business and research until we left after lunch for Botlek.

As I clambered towards my cabin when joining that first night, the repeated plethora of safety notices situated around the tanker registered in my mind. They appeared in alleyways, on various bulkheads throughout the ship, on the main deck, in the engine-room, the wheelhouse and every personal cabin.

I supposed this being a smaller ship than *Anna Knutsen* they appeared to be more frequent in comparatively smaller spaces. The notices resulted from careful thought and were attractively eye-catching with immediate visual impact. The most impressive and important was BP Shipping's admonition to every person on board inviting them to 'Take Five'. The versatility of 'Take Five' stresses the approach BP Shipping expects their employees to adopt *before* undertaking *any* job in *every* department aboard ship. It presents the closest to a blueprint that is possible for

The senior table in the dining room with the Master and chief engineer immediately to starboard and port respectively, with other seats taken by the chief officer and second engineer (Author's Collection).

The officers' lounge incorporated a wide collection of video films–some new titles were bought in the Botlek stores by the Master–together with an assortment of books, magazines, computer games, DVDs and audio CDs. It was a place where off-duty officers could unwind in comfortable armchairs and enjoy a few moments of relaxation in between watches (Author's Collection).

encouraging thought before action safely and efficiently. To me, the posters collectively emphasised not merely safety, but the *ethos* of safety that permeated so naturally part of daily life aboard both the shuttle tanker and *British Ensign*. I instinctively found myself opening doors with more focussed attention in case someone else was entering at the same moment, or even passing.

Following her second partial discharge the tanker was due to shift berth and to complete offloading at another oil-haven in Europoort. It was encouraging to see that the unpredictability of life at sea remained undiminished, for *British Ensign* was delayed an extra day by 'limited shore crew availability'—a delightful euphemism implying the mooring gang was required elsewhere, having seemingly been double-booked or, alternatively, being

The plain message of 'Take Five' lacked the visual immediacy of many safety posters situated in strategic places aboard all BP tankers. It was its lack of coloured animation which emphasised the impact–for the five points illustrated conveyed the entire safety philosophy advocated by this Company, expected from each of their seafaring employees–and, by transference, to all visitors to their tankers (Author's Collection).

Safety posters situated aboard all BP tankers encouraging seafarers and visitors to their ships to consider the importance of personal safety–as well as that of others.

above: A brightly coloured poster placed in the engine-room (where 85% of all shipboard accidents occur).

far left: The 'ostrich approach to safety' poster in the dining room.

left: Poster on companionway bulkhead.

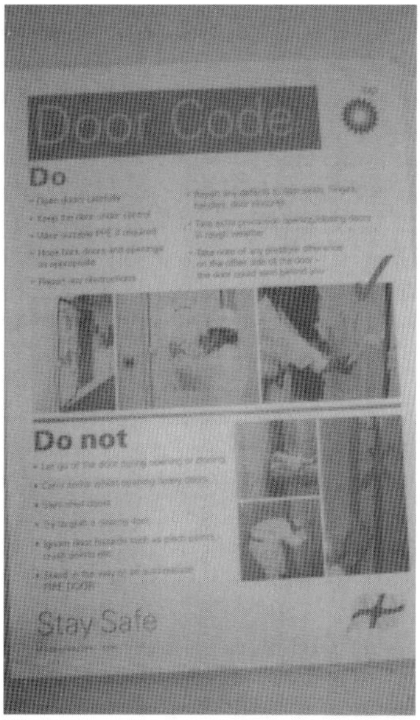

Further posters on companionway bulkheads and in alleyways (all Author's Collection).

Safe Working Load (swl) limits painted on deck and bitts (Author's Collection).

the only gang available for duty. These might appear major problems, but in the colossal administration required to work one of the world's largest oil ports, it requires only one man along the line to report sick, leaving the finding of replacements at extremely short notice an impossible task. This incident exemplified the kind of difficulty experienced anywhere in the world. I could not help reflecting that 'accountants had their way' yet again in their quest for economic viability for, in 'yesteryear' spare hands would have been on call as standby men at comparatively short notice. It proved an ill wind—and ample time was certainly available for the promised visit to Botlek Stores. This was completed successfully and along with new trousers, shirts, plus a present for my wife—and a handy-sized pair of binoculars, my equilibrium was regained. We later shifted to the other side of the berth and after a few hours' cargo work sailed to Number Four Petrol Harbour to complete discharge. A further two-day wait was caused by another vessel delayed on the berth for which we had been booked.

I observed the conference between Master, Chief Officer, agent and shore cargo surveyor called following notification to the terminal that cargo operations were approaching completion. The cargo surveyor verified the vessel had discharged her naptha cargo. Once terminal and vessel had agreed figures, the agent delivered his port clearance certificate to the Master, serving as authority for the ship to sail. It was then that the preliminary booking for tugs and pilot was confirmed, and shortly before their arrival 'stand by' was called, enabling officers and crew to go to stations for leaving harbour. By this time, the Chiksans® had been disconnected, manifolds secured and made oil-tight, with any loose cargo gear used stowed into the appropriate lockers.

British Ensign was proceeding in ballast for her next cargo, so the sequence of events covering her departure followed established regulated routines designed for safety and efficiency aboard any tanker. Simultaneously with cargo discharge, sea water had been taken into the Segregated Ballast Tanks (SBT), ensuring sufficient weight in the vessel for propeller and rudder to function efficiently. Ballast water also proportioned stresses along the ship's hull, assisting safe stability for the forthcoming voyage. This helped the vessel 'ride' waves correctly without excess pitching and rolling in normal seas. During this stage, if crude oil had been carried, tanks would have been selected for Crude Oil Washing—under IGS protection—using fixed automatic tank washing machines to remove virtually all cargo, reduce sediment in the vessel's tanks, and decrease time on the berth. Tanks are cleaned according to a carefully planned schedule on a rota basis.

Shortly before arrival of pilot and tugs, officers on duty in the wheelhouse and engine-room tested all equipment to ensure it remained in good working order, in much the same way as an aeroplane tests its equipment before take-off. The work involved engaging the telemotor as necessary and shifting the steering wheel 35 degrees hard a-port to hard a-starboard ensuring freedom of movement devoid of jamming. Other duties included thorough testing of communication systems, engine telegraph, radars and gyro and magnetic compasses. Correct alignment was made to compass repeaters, with navigational equipment, helm indicators and navigation lights being checked. Times were synchronised between deck and engine-room clocks to enable consistency in recording telegraph movements. Among other duties, the Movement Book was prepared for use, into which would be recorded names of pilot/tugs, and whether the latter were made fast or in attendance, plus any other events significant to departure. The engineer officers, meanwhile, warmed through the main engine, checking that sufficient air existed in the starting-bottle. The engine was turned over on air to ensure that it would be free to move when required. All of these tests followed mandatory checklists, the results of which were recorded in deck and engine-room logbooks.

With the arrival of the pilot in the wheelhouse, a further checklist was completed ensuring correct procedures for departure. He was provided with a pilot information card giving details of the ship's capabilities under our appropriate ballasted condition. By this time, the crew had been called to stations and the vessel singled up to one head line and a stern line. With tugs fast fore and aft, the vessel let go all moorings to the terminal and commenced her outward voyage. During the pilotage passage, mooring ropes were stowed below decks, any loose equipment secured and cargo tanks double-checked to ascertain they were secure. By now, as time permitted, the anchors were housed in the hawse pipe, with the cable made fast by applying 'guillotines' or 'devil's claws', whilst the spurling pipe (where the anchor chain enters the deck to the cable locker) was covered with tarpaulin and cement to eliminate water ingress to the chain locker during possible bad weather encountered on the voyage. Even if not used, anchors were always cleared on arrival being walked out of the hawse pipe in readiness for potential emergencies.

Certainly, passing Europoort once more brought its own myriad of personal memories. After we had dropped the pilot' with the vessel checked visually and by all other means and seen to be clear of danger, the officer-of-the-watch reported to the bridge, whilst the standby Mate, and Master—as appropriate in the light of traffic density and conditions—stood down.

bp PILOT INFORMATION CARD

M/T BRITISH ENSIGN CALL SIGN: MMER9

PORT: ROTTERDAM DATE: 06TH NOV. 06

DRAUGHT: FWD: 5.8 m ______ ft AFT: 7.7 m ______ ft

AIR DRAUGHT: 37.81 m ______ ft YEAR BUILT: 2006

SUMMER DEADWEIGHT: 36713.0 tonnes DISPLACEMENT: 27086 MT

SHIP'S PARTICULARS

Length Overall: 184.22 m
Breadth: 27.40 m
Bulbous bow: Y

Anchor Chain: **Port: 11 Shackles** **Starboard: 11 Shackles**
STERN: N/A
(1 shackle = 27.5m / 15 fathoms)

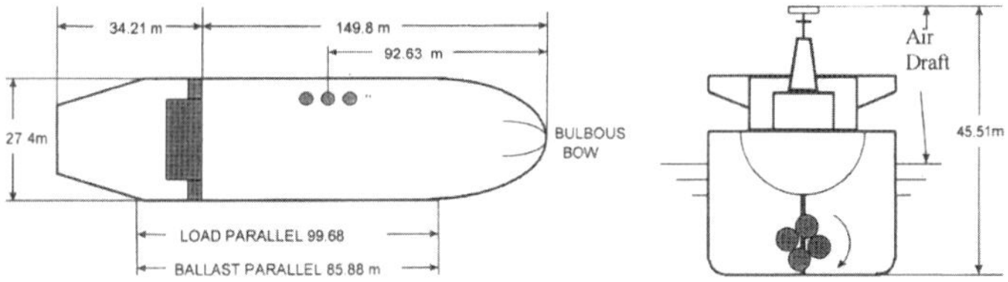

ENGINE **MAXIMUM POWER:**

MANOEUVRING ENGINE ORDER	RPM	SPEED (Knots) LOADED	SPEED (Knots) BALLAST
FULL AHEAD	**105**	**13.40**	**13.65**
HALF AHEAD	**85**	**10.75**	**10.97**
SLOW AHEAD	**64**	**8.18**	**8.37**
DEAD SLOW AHEAD	**45**	**5.70**	**5.87**
DEAD SLOW ASTERN	**- 45**		
SLOW ASTERN	**- 64**		
HALF ASTERN	**- 85**		
FULL ASTERN	**- 105**		

FULL AHEAD TO FULL ASTERN: LOADED: ms BALLAST: ms

STOPPING DISTANCES (HARBOUR FULL): LOADED: Nm ms BALLAST: Nm ms

TIME LIMIT ASTERN **Min**

MAX NUMBER OF CONSECUTIVE STARTS: 12

MINIMUM CONTINUOUS RPM: 31.3 rpm Kts

POWER OUTPUT ASTERN: %

The first of three pages representing the Pilot Information Card of the *British Ensign* covering her shifting berth from Europoort to Petroleum Harbour Number Four, showing essential information concerning the tanker's manoeuvrability and performance. The eventual departure draught was 5.8 metres forward and 7.7-metre aft, with an air draught of 37.81-metre - the latter required for under-bridge clearances where appropriate (BP Shipping).

STEERING PARTICULARS

Type of Rudder: ....SEMI BALANCED SPADE TYPE..

Maximum Angle: ....35.. °

Rudder Area: .... m^2

Hard-over to Hard-over: ....24 sec with one power unit...14 sec with two power unit

Rudder Angle for Neutral Effect: .... 0°

Thruster: ....YES...

CHECKED IF ABOARD AND READY

Anchors	✓	Indicators:	
Whistle	✓	Rudder	✓
Radar .... 3 cm	✓ 10 cm ✓	RPM	✓
ARPA	✓	Rate of Turn	✓
Speed Log	✓ Doppler: Yes / ~~No~~	Compass System	✓
Water Speed	✓	Constant Gyro Error .... +/- - 0.5 °	
Ground Speed	✓	VHF	✓
Engine Telegraphs	✓	Elec. Pos. Fix. System	✓
Steering Gear	✓	Type ...... D GPS	
Number of Steering Gears' Power Units Operating	2		

OTHER INFORMATION:

MASTER: ______________ (SIGNATURE)

PILOT (1): ______________ (SIGNATURE)

PILOT (2): ______________ (SIGNATURE)

M.T.BRITISH ENSIGN

CALL SIGN	MMER9
FLAG	ISLE OF MAN
PORT OF REGISTRY	DOUGLAS
OFFICIAL NUMBER	DR 134
IMO/LLOYDS NUMBER	9312913
CLASS SOCIETY	LR
CLASS NOTATION	100A1 DOUBLE HULL OIL TANKER ,ESP,LI, *IWS,SPM, ICE CLASS 1A, FS
P & I CLUB	STANDARD STEAMSHIP OWNER P&I ASSOC.(Bermuda)

KEEL LAID	05-Dec-05
LAUNCHED	07-Mar-06
DELIVERED	26-Apr-06
SHIPYARD	HYUNDAI MIPO DOCK, ULSAN, SOUTH KOREA

SATELLITE COMMUNICATION		
	INMARSAT-F	FLEET 33
PHONE	764624157	
FAX	764624158	
INM-C TLX	423500999	
ANS BACK	ENSI X	
MMSI	235010980	
E-mail	britishensign@bpfleet.com	

OWNERS	SHIPPING RIDER COMPANY, Marshall Island Trust Co Complex, Ajeltake Rd., Ajeltake Island, Majuro, MARSHALL ISLANDS
OPERATORS	BP SHIPPING LIMITED, Chertsey Road, Sunbury On Thames, Middlesex TW16 7LN, UK

PRINCIPAL DIMENSIONS	
LOA	184.22
LBP	176
BREADTH (Extreme)	27.4
DEPTH (moulded)	17.2
HEIGHT (maximum)	45.51
BRIDGE FRONT - BOW	149.48
BRIDGE FRONT - STERN	34.74 M
BRIDGE FRONT - M'FOLD	56.85

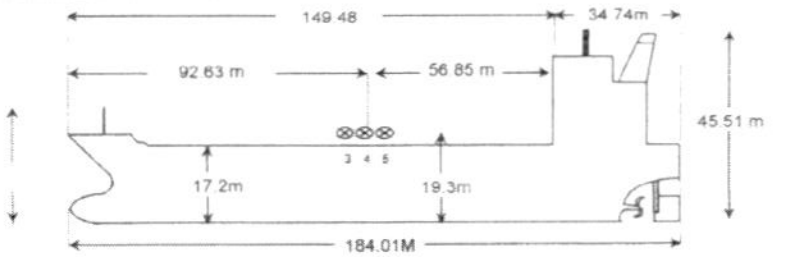

TONNAGE	REGD	SUEZ
NET	9925	
GROSS	23270	
GROSS Reduced (R'n:13495)		

LOAD LINE INFORMATION	FREEBOARD	DRAFT	DWT
TROPICAL FRESH	5.425	11.804	37754.0
FRESH	5.66	11.569	36714.0
TROPICAL	5.678	11.551	37774.0
SUMMER	5.913	11.316	36713.0
WINTER	6.148	11.081	35652.0
LIGHTSHIP	14.56	2.648	8915.0
NORMAL BALLAST COND	10.589	6.640	16530.0
SEG. BALLAST COND	10.449	6.780	17,091.0

TANK CAPACITIES (cbm)					
CARGO TANKS (98 %)				BLST TKS (100 %)	
COT 1P	2531.5	COT 1S	2531.5	F.P.Tk.	601.6
COT 2P	3561.2	COT 2S	3561.2	WBT 1P	1446.6
COT 3P	3621.8	COT 3S	3621.8	WBT 1S	1210.2
COT 4P	3627.2	COT 4S	3627.2	WBT 2P	1424.9
COT 5P	3620.2	COT 5S	3620.2	WBT 2S	1188.5
COT 6P	3329.0	COT 6S	3329.0	WBT 3P	1074.2
TOTAL EXCL. SLOPS	40581.8	SLOP P	516	WBT 3S	1074.2
		SLOP S	516	WBT 4P	1074.3
G.TOTAL	41613.8	TOTAL SLP	1032	WBT 4S	1074.3
OTHER DETAILS		FRESH WATER (cbm)		WBT 5P	1055.9
FWA	253mm	FWT P	124.6	WBT 5S	1055.9
TPC@Summer	45.1	FWT S	76.9	WBT 6P	1689.9
Overfill Alarm		DRINK S	47.7	WBT 6S	1429.1
		tech fw	270.1	3c	1875.6
Level Gauge		TOTAL FW	519.3	AFT Pk.	236.1
High Level Alm				TOTAL	17511.3

MACHINERY / PROPELLER / RUDDER	
MAIN ENGINE	HYUNDAI-B&W 6S50MC-c
M.C.R.	12900BHPX127RPM
N.C.R.	10965BHPX120.3RPM
MAX CR RANGE	
AUX. BOILER	1 vertical cyl water tube type
GENERATOR (3 sets)	HYUNDAI HINSEN
PROPELLER	4 Blade/Fixed
RUDDER	Semi Balanced, Hanging Type
STEERING GEAR	ROTARY VANE
FW GENERATOR CAP	20 TON/DAY
HYD.POWER PACK	

BUNKER TANKS98%	
FOT (P)	483.30
FOT (S)	306.40
HFO Set.	41.00
HFO Srv	54.60
LSFO (S)	254.20
TOTAL	1139.50
MGO (P)	83.40
MGO (S)	48.10
MGO Set.	0.00
MGO Srv	35.40
TOTAL	166.90

WINCHES / WINDLASS / ROPES / EMERGENCY TOWING			
	FRD	AFT	PARTICULARS
WINCHES	6	6	split Drum,15T,15m/Min,Frctn Band Brake
MRG WIRES	6	6	Steel Wire6x37, 28mm, 200 m, B.S 51T
Winch BHL			40.8ts
WINDLASS	2		
FIRE WIRE	1	1	GSWR 6x37, 28mm x 45 mtrs
ANCHOR	2		11 shackles each
EMG. TOWING	1		Bow Chain Stopper - Tongue Type
			SWL 200T, Chafing Chain 76mm x 8m
		1	ETS 2000A-SJ, SWL Closed Chock - 100T

CARGO AND BALLAST PUMPING SYSTEM				
MAIN PUMPS	NO.	CAPACITY	HEAD	RPM
COP'S 1 WINGS	2	300 CUB.M/HR	130	
COP'S SLOPS	2	150 CUB.M/HR	130	
BALLAST PUMP	2	750 CUB.M/HR	25 m	
PORTABLE FRAMO	1	150 CUB.M/HR	130	
TANK CLNG PUMP	1	100 CUB.M/HR	110 m	
COP'S 2-6 Wings	10	500Cum/HR	130	
FIRE/GS PUMP	2	R	90/30	
EMG.FIRE PUMP	1	72 CUB.M/HR	80 m	

LIFE BOATS	
1 FFLB X 30 PERS	
LIFE RAFTS	
4x16 P, 1x6P	
TK CLNG MCHN	
1 PER TK	40 Cub.m/Hr
CRANES	
Hose Crane	10 T
Prov. Crane	2 T
Res.Boat Davit	

MANIFOLD ARRANGEMENT (400 mm / Steel)	
Distance of cargo manifold to cargo manifold	2000 mm
Distance of cargo manifold to vpr. return manifold	2000 mm
Distance of manifolds to ship's rail	4500 mm
Distance of spill tray grating to centre of manifold	900 mm
Distance of main deck to centre of manifold	2100 mm
Distance of main deck to top of rail	1390mm
Distance of top of rail to centre of manifold	710mm
Distance of manifold to ship side	4600 mm
Distance of manifold from keel	19.3

IG / VAPOUR EMISSION / VENTING	
I.G BLOWER CAPACITY (2 nos)	3750CuM/HR
P/V VALVE PR./ VAC. SETTING	2000/-350 mmwg
P/V BREAKER PR./VAC. SETTING	2300/-700 mmwg

Min Bow Drft:	
Blst Drft:	
G.Blst Drft:	
Propeller Immersion:	

FIRE FIGHTING SYSTEM	
E/RM	CO2 / Local hyper mist system
CARGO AREA	Low exp. foam 3 % Fluor Foamousse,3500L
PAINT STORE	Water Sprinkler

The following four photographs show the approaches to Rotterdam and Europoort and make a comparison between the chart display and the observed view and capture admirably something of the essence of this departure.

View from the wheelhouse as *British Ensign* leaves Europoort (Author's Collection).

The electronic chart display (see p.76) on *British Ensign* shows the track of the ship as two concentric circles. The course of the ship appears on the electronic chart system as a double-arrowed vector showing forecast movement in six minutes. The tanker has just cleared the light structure on the starboard quarter indicating the junction separating the two very distinct and separate channel exits from the deep-draught channel for very large tankers and bulk carriers, from that which leads into Rotterdam. The Noorderdam Tower marking the northern limit of the dredged channel, with its structure marking the port side limit, are being approached on the starboard side. In the photograph, the mid-channel tower is being approached and the port hand CA2 buoy very close to it, and the starboard hand Maas 5 and Maas 3 buoys off the port bow, below the wind farm, can each be clearly identified from the chart display. An incoming vessel off the starboard bow of *British Ensign* partially hides the northern light structure, but the southern limit 'tower' is visible fine off the port bow. Just astern of the mid-channel tower, the NW1 buoy is identifiable.

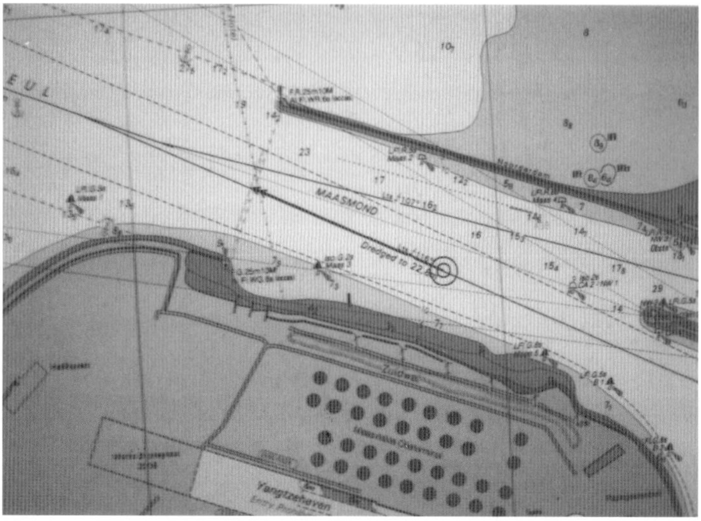

British Ensign approaches the light-tower (Author's Collection).

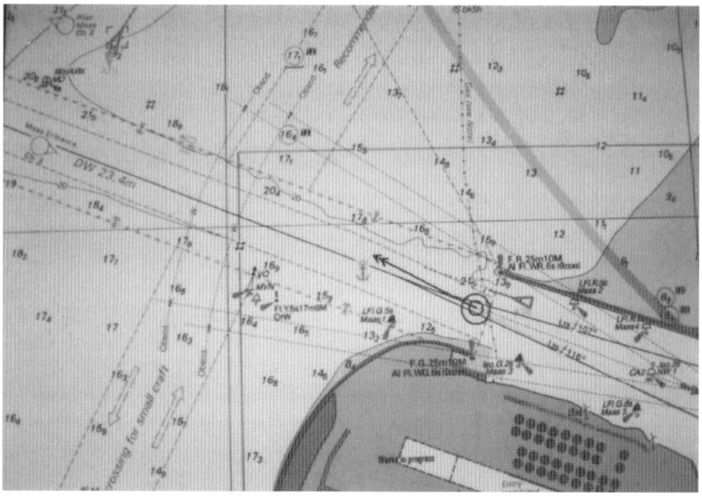

The tanker with the light-tower on her starboard beam. The wind farm symbols are just visible above the black circles of the oil terminal (Author's Collection).

The chart display above indicates the tanker clearing the harbour exit limits and shows also the position of other ships, whilst the vector offers an indication of their course and speed. The vessel just abaft the starboard beam is an overtaking small chemical tanker, whilst the triangle in the top left-hand side off the starboard bow indicates another larger tanker dropping her pilot at the Maas Pilot Station. The size of targets cannot be deduced from the size of the triangle for this indicates merely the presence of another target.

A reassuring reflection of traditional practice–Master, Captain Jagdip Singh Gill automatically picks up the binoculars to check 'something ahead' as he cons his ship out of the Rotterdam approaches. A duty quartermaster is placed on the helm for greater immediate control of the ship prior to putting the tanker to automatic pilot for the passage run. The backs of the three screens in the foreground are the Electronic Chart Display Information System (ECDIS) and the 10- and 3-cm radar sets (Author's Collection).

With the pilot safely in his cutter, and *British Ensign* set to her pre-planned course from the lee created for the safety of the pilot vessel, Full Away on Passage was indicated to the engine-room and noted in the logbook. A gradual almost imperceptible increase in vibration indicated a slow build-up of revolutions on the main engine from full ahead manoeuvring to full sea speed. Prior to sailing, the Second Officer had completed safe passage planning covering the voyage from berth to berth. This had been approved by the Master and signed by each officer responsible for the passage navigation watches. All required charts, light lists, and radio signals had been checked onboard, and corrected up to date from the latest electronic weekly notices to mariners and navigational warnings. I had previously been in the wheelhouse whilst the second mate had prepared his voyage plan, and he had talked aspects of this through using updated small-scale British Admiralty (BA) 5124 and the larger-scale BA 2128B routeing charts, together with company recommendations and advice, planning our passage towards Skagen in Denmark. From Skagen, the ship would take a pilot and continue south down the Skagerrak towards our loading port Gulfhaven. During the early stages, the duty Mate settled to traditional patterns of watch keeping, assisted by a rating who acted as lookout, and helmsman when required.

The route being followed conformed to shortest distances, taking into account as appropriate effects of weather routeing advice, strength and direction of currents, traffic density, depth of water under the keel, available navigational aids with allowances made for contingency plans in the event of an emergency. The head office superintendents also stipulate and advise appropriate action determinate upon geographic location and certain conditions. Consistent with all modern tankers, *British Ensign* was equipped with a range of electronic aids to navigation, and the Master, Chief Engineer, and all officers and ratings were fully qualified in accordance with STCW95 covering international regulations for certification. In addition, senior deck officers held a recognised Dangerous Cargo Endorsement (DCE) to their certificates of competency. Much of the ship's gear was supplied by the Japan Radio Company (JRC), including both radars—the

The Hyundai Bridge Control Unit gave telephone communication to the engine-room and other stations aboard ship, together with direct engine telegraph control. Situated at the far end of the console is the secondary radar. Japan Radio company two-way VHF receiver/transmitters for use during berthing and other operations may be seen on the ledge in front of the windows (Author's Collection).

The Yokogawa automatic pilot and steering wheel was fitted with off-course alarms and adjustment controls to provide greater accuracy in steering making allowances for wind and tidal conditions. The system allowed also for manual steering during berthing operations, and at other times when a greater degree of control was required over the ship's manoeuvring. Often, for example, it was useful to have a rating on the wheel when passing another ship at close quarters. The gear provided was similar to that found aboard numerous ocean-going and coastal ships and it never ceased to amaze me that a 300,000 s-dwt tanker, for example, could have minor adjustments made to her course merely by moving appropriately the small black control knob fitted in the centre of the upper dial (Author's Collection).

3-cm 'S' and 10-cm 'X' wavelength, of which the 10-cm was equipped also with ARPA (Automatic Radar Plotting Aid) function as a computer-controlled aid to collision avoidance. This set was equipped with the AIS (Automatic Identification System) already encountered aboard the Knutsen tanker. Other navigational aids and electronic equipment on the bridge included JRC Digital GPS, JRC Navtex echo-sounder receiver, electronic Doppler logs, helm and rate of turn indicators, Yokogawa autopilot and gyro-compass with azimuth mirror, JRC weather facsimile receiver and safety equipment, and JRC's Global Maritime Distress and Safety System (GMDSS) communications console. A Hyundai Bridge Control Unit completed the impressive modern equipment. GMDSS was not only an aid to navigation, but provided reliable and safe communication to the shore and other vessels. On this ship, a number of these electronic aids were linked into an Integrated Bridge System. There were also course recorders, bridge control systems of the main engine, and a second gyro and magnetic compasses. These were complemented by fire detection and fire extinguishing activation systems with back-ups and power supply alarms activated in the event of any systems failure.

My experiences on the *British Ensign* were similar to those aboard *Anna Knutsen* for, once at sea, I found evidence again of a limited social fabric. Most off-duty personnel kept to their cabins, resting in preparation for future watches, and there was again that almost *Mary Celeste* feel of a ship's accommodation devoid of crew. Although this BP ship did not have a swimming pool, she was well equipped with off-duty facilities for the crew, including digital television and video, stereos, table tennis, library and various computer games. A modern well-equipped gymnasium was available, again with instructions designed for safe use, and advice enabling maximum benefit to be derived from the facilities. The Company permitted all crew to have a free 20-minute phone call by satellite link each day with their families, and a computer was set up in the Conference Room for instant email access home.

It was interesting and rewarding to speak with various ranks on board and learn how they reacted to their chosen life at sea. The majority were enthusiastic and dedicated to their work. This

Rather Spartan in appearance perhaps, but the main conference room was equipped with email linked computer allowing instant access to families anywhere in the world, together with a bulkhead telephone upon which the Company permitted all crew-members and visitors a free 20-minute call daily (Author's Collection).

crew also recognised the need for safety and did not appear to regard having to follow stipulated procedures in any way irksome. Probably, this was because most newcomers had been inculcated in the 'right way to do a job' with induction courses prior to joining a first ship and regarded following safety procedures as very much the norm. Older officers and crew had recognised the inevitable, put the past behind them and either conformed, or exercised their option and left the industry. There was one youngster who seemed to be having difficulties adjusting to life at sea. How he would respond after this, his first voyage, with his seven-month tour completed was impossible to predict. An ethos prevailed that provided all possible help—and I witnessed the surreptitious kindness afforded him by all ranks—but the decision whether or not he would return remained very much his own. I have often wondered what that turned out to be!

The pattern of watchkeeping followed traditional formats of all merchant ships at sea: with a working day for those on watch, or keeping the day-routines averaging around ten to twelve hours. Watchkeepers spend eight hours on watch, split into four-hour periods, during which the navigating officer is confined to the bridge at all times and cannot leave his or her post unless relieved by another qualified bridge watchkeeper. Toilet and hand-washing facilities are immediately handy. Kettles with ample tea and coffee are also available. The maintenance work for which that officer is responsible has to be performed outside his watchkeeping duties. The recognised daily navigating watchkeeping remained as follows: 0800 to 1200 hours and 2000 to 0000 hours saw the Third Officer on the bridge. This has always been a traditional scenario, allowing newly qualified mates the majority of daylight hours on the bridge. It invariably coincides also with the more ready availability of the Master during morning and evening hours—although that senior officer responsible for his ship expects to be called to the bridge by any officer of any seniority during occasions of need. The Third Mate is responsible also for all life-saving appliances (LSA) on board including checking of safety and lifeboats. The mate is responsible to the Master for safe navigational planning of the ship, the Second Officer keeps the 1200 to 1600 hours and the 0000 to 0400 hours watches, whilst the Chief Officer responsible for all loading and discharging, ship deck maintenance and deck crew organisation and control has the 0400 to 0800 hours and 1600 to 2000 hours watches. Quarters and facilities on this ship for the crew were impressive, as expected from a leading tanker operator, and were certainly comparable with those on the Knutsen shuttle tanker. Each, from Master to lowest rating had an en-suite cabin, which facilitated considerably the accomodation of female officers and crew, although there were none carried on this particular trip. Whilst all 24 crew aboard *British Ensign* were Indians, it is not out of the ordinary to have mixed nationality crews on board. On these occasions, however, it is compulsory for the crew to share a common language (usually English) not only to communicate in the routine running of the ship but, more importantly, to respond effectively in any emergency.

The intensive work by the vessel's officers continued whilst the BP tanker was at sea. A quiet passage experienced during our run up the North-European coast towards the Kattegat, with the ship pitching and rolling easily, enabled some routine maintenance work to be carried out. These duties had been planned during a previous voyage conference and were posted daily outside the officers' and crew mess decks in a polythene folder fitted to the bulkhead so that each day-man knew precisely where he would be working and what was expected of him. The lists covered a range of eventualities such as maintenance and practice in the use of fire-fighting and life-saving equipment, safety routines, onboard training and navigational and engineering duties. It was good to be reminded that all services supplied ashore had to be provided by the ship's engineering department. These included hot and cold fresh water, sewage treatment plant, heating and/or air conditioning, cooling services for the ship's storerooms and fridges, electrical supplies for lighting, navigational equipment, deck, engine and galley machinery, heating supplies for the fuel oil and/or cargo, and deck service supplies such as seawater, air, hydraulic oil, fresh water and steam. To use an analogy, if the bridge was the 'brain' of the vessel, the engine-room remained very much its 'heart'—and one department could not operate

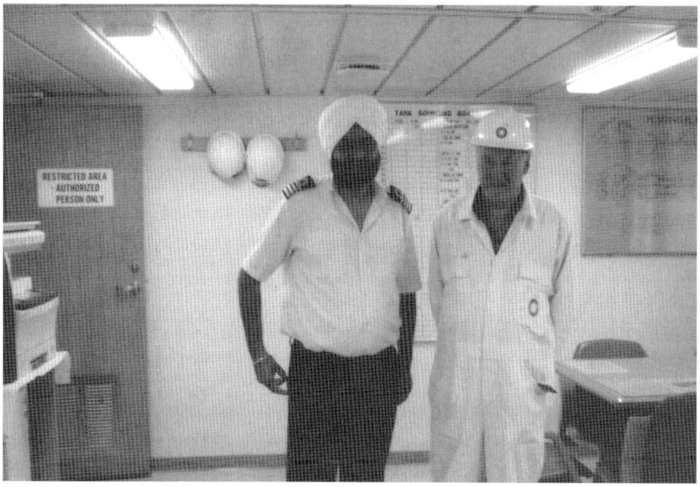

The Master and author in front of the tank sounding board with the loading/discharging conference table and vessel pumping plan to starboard (Author's Collection).

The cargo control room equipment, which consisted of varied displays enabling cargo to be loaded and discharged in complete safety. The state of the tanks and condition of all valves could be seen at all times with the valves opened or closed by finger touch. The levels and temperatures in all tanks were recorded by tank radar beam measurements using a parabolic beam operating on measured differences between a transmitted and reflected signal. Tank overfill alarms systems operated, and the vessel was fitted with a cargo planning system which offered reliable and accurate information concerning actual shearing forces and bending moment conditions throughout the tanks and hull. The control room was fitted additionally with a range of computerised information programs, rapid communication systems throughout the tanker, and a colour photocopier. It was at a table near the door that cargo planning discussions with shore superintendents took place (Author's Collection).

without the other. All seafarers received training in sea survival, fire-fighting and life-saving appliances. An onboard safety training programme took place weekly (weather permitting) consisting of pollution response drills, theoretical lifeboat launching procedures, and often fire drills (at the manifold, in the accommodation and engine-room). There were also the routine drills found aboard all tankers covering cargo release, man-overboard, emergency steering, and likely action responses to catastrophic accidents such as collision, grounding, and pump-room rescue. When weather prevented such drills taking place they were often replaced with training lectures from ship's officers in the use of distress signals, self-contained breathing apparatus equipment, escape equipment, and safety training videos. All such drills were entered in the ship's logbook for inspection by Port State Control and the company's ship management auditing officer. The engine was usually unmanned at night while at sea. This period, known as UMS (unmanned machinery space), is permitted only when the engine-room meets stringent requirements, including the provision of alarm systems in the event of any problems occurring. One engineer is assigned the Duty Engineer each night to attend the engine-room in case of any alarms. Otherwise all engineers worked in the engine-room during the day and were responsible for maintenance and operation of different engine-room equipment in accordance with their planned maintenance system.

After the COW procedure following a crude oil cargo discharge, the machines were available during the ballast passage to water wash the tanks, should entry be required or in preparation for a next cargo. Tank inspections on this vessel were not so vital at this early stage in her life, although a programme was already under discussion for future development. On this ship, when each crude oil cargo was loaded, tanks were cleaned and the residue retained in the designated slop tanks. Subject to the inevitable pitching and rolling of the vessel whilst underway, the residual oil was permitted to settle to such limits that the majority of the old cargo floated on top of the water. The water only was then discharged into the sea in strict accordance with MARPOL regulations through the Overboard Discharge Monitoring Equipment (ODME), reducing the quantity of slops remaining onboard on arrival at the next load port, and ascertaining no oil was discharged into the sea. This regulation was rigidly enforced on board—and taken very seriously. If the next cargo proved compatible, this would then be loaded on top of these slops in an established procedure known as the 'load-on-top' (LOT) system; it would otherwise be landed ashore.

It was both inevitable and encouraging to find strict adherence aboard *British Ensign* to the International Safety Management codes with similar fervency to that found aboard *Anna Knutsen*. A range of Shipboard Management Safety systems (SMS) retains an important role aboard all vessels and are taken seriously. This provides for more efficient use of available resources and has a corresponding impact on safe and efficient operations. I saw the practical results on both vessels—with professionally applied integrated training programmes implementing courses undertaken ashore. It was argued that IT software could be geared to supplement and reinforce the work of seafarers by even *reducing* the amount of paperwork involved. SMS aboard BP Shipping and Knutsen OAS ships permits the exercise of considerable freedom when implementing management codes. Senior seagoing officers in all departments are encouraged to develop their own approaches and support the efforts of the ship's 'designated person' by discussion and consultation. Inevitably, any new system—even one in use for a decade or so—will continue to experience unique 'teething troubles', and much remains to be done as slimmer and more cost-effective implementation is sought. Arguably, the situation is not always consistently eased by the varying standards applied between flag-state administrations and (to date) it has not always been possible for universal standards to operate across the complete range of shipboard practices. For example, some flag states and port-monitoring authorities may well accept digital copies of some practices, whilst others would insist on hard copies also being available. The Master mentioned a report he had heard in this respect where one flag state refused to allow GPS deep-sea celestial positions to be used without a chart back-up taken by the now virtually archaic sextant observations, whilst most others were quite happy to accept the former alone. It is certain that eventually a consistent code will emerge across all areas of shipboard safety and pollution control, and it was found encouraging that many positive steps are being taken in order to achieve this goal.

BP Shipping operates or time charters around 150 tankers at any time and, recently, has carried 251.7 million tonnes of cargo on 6,902 voyages without accident or spills into the environment. Its Clean Seas Seven-Point Charter, established in 2005, determined the Company's commitment to remain a leader in fields of environmental protection, through safe operating practices—including recruitment of competently professional crews—and promoting consistency of awareness throughout the organisation. In practical terms, this has committed BP Shipping to following a rigid Health, Safety and Environmental (HSE) performance policy, which remains class inclusive from the Group Chief Executive or Chairman of the company to the most menial employee—and all ranks in between. The message delivered from the chief executive stood in plain unambiguous language—and was unequivocal: *'Everybody who works for BP, anywhere, is responsible for getting HSE right. Good HSE performance and the health, safety and security of everyone who works for us are critical to the success of our business. Our goals are simply stated - no accidents, no harm to people, and no damage to the environment'.* Success was achievable, and practised by following active policies of consulting, listening

The Thirteen Elements of BP's HSE Management System Framework designed to ensure a safe working environment where concern for the safety of others was ranked equally with personal safety, by following a series of Expectations based on a simple but effective Statement of Achievement (BP Group).

Thirteen Elements of BP's HSE Management System Framework

1. Leadership and Accountability
2. Risk Assessment and Management
3. People Training and Behaviour
4. Working with Contractors and Others
5. Facilities Design and Construction
6. Operations and Maintenance
7. Management of Change
8. Information and documentation
9. Customers and Products
10. Community and Stakeholder Awareness
11. Crisis and Emergency Management
12. Incidents Analysis and Prevention
13. Assessment, Assurance and Improvement

Delivering HSE Assurance

Assurance is the process whereby Business Unit and Support Unit Managers confirm that processes are in place and working effectively in order to manage the key internal controls for, and major risks to, sustainable business performance. This process is supplemented periodically by an unbiased Assurance Audit.

HSE Assurance addresses delivery of:

- BP's HSE Commitment
- HSE Expectations
- legal compliance

HSE Assurance is a continuous review process involving regular dialogues about:

- supporting Assurance Audit, Peer and Business Unit Assessments
- identifying and managing risks
- evaluating HSE performance trends

These are documented in a formal Annual HSE Report.

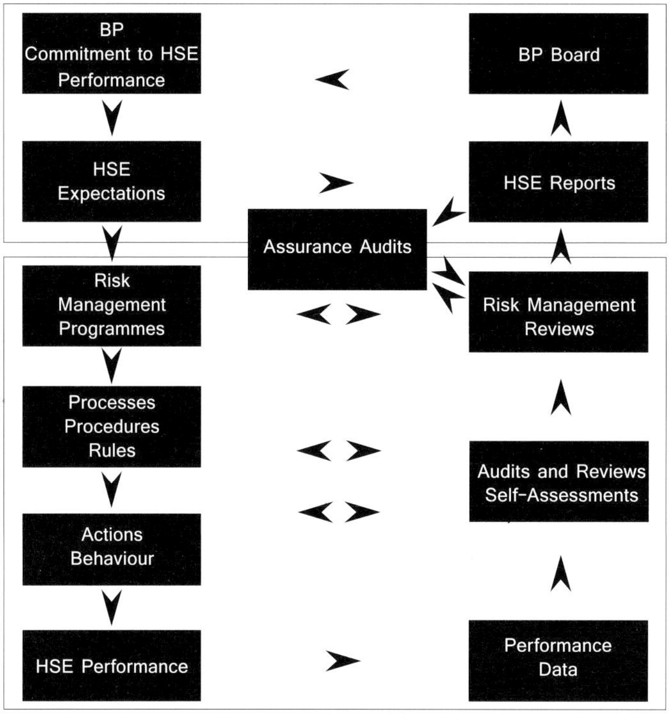

The flow diagram indicates the way in which the various management systems inter-relate and involve employees in all levels of circumstances and relationships, working and co-operating together (BP Group)

Three views showing the engine control console and main six-cylinder Hyundai-B&W engine and crankcase (Author's Collection).

and responding at all levels and with all relevant sources; by measuring performance and recognising areas where these fell short—and then discussing methods of improvement. The Company encouraged involvement in thirteen elements (see page 88), which were proposed, examined and then delivered in the form of a series of clear Expectations. Working through a range of HSE management systems, the Company offered a process by which management at every level was equipped to deliver sustainable business performances ashore and at sea. HSE remains a serious business operating at all levels and branches constituting the BP Group, ashore and afloat, with continuous review systems instituted, and performances regularly assessed. The implications on board all of the Company's tankers permeated every level of work and even places of relaxation in a series of basic, common-sense approaches, resulting in adherence to safe practices, in all areas of shipboard life.

Equipped in boiler suit, boots, helmet and safety goggles, I took the opportunity during this quiet stage of passage-making to accept the long-pressed Chief Engineer's invitation to 'pop along to his domain'. Again, the immediate impression was the cleanliness of all areas visited, the plethora of safety notices encountered, and the modern state-of-the-art technology. The main engine was a six-cylinder Hyundai-B&W, and there were three sets of generators.

British Ensign took bunkers and a pilot off Skagen in Denmark. The second mate's passage plan covered all aspects of the near-45-mile second leg to Gulfhaven. Delay was experienced on arrival at Stignaes owing to another tanker on the berth being late in completing loading, but instead of anchoring, we had earlier reduced speed resulting in a safe passing of this vessel just before approaching our berth. Gulfhaven is Stignaes' oil pier, an old established discharge port I recall

Chart-table with chart just showing the area of Gulfhaven and the bridge crossing the fairway under which all ships entering the port from the north have to pass. GPS Navigator and weather facsimile receivers, together with the NavTex, and echo sounder recorders are amongst the monitors above the chart. On the far side is the GMDSS communications console with its Immarsat Mobil Earth Satellite station (Author's Collection).

visiting on a coastal tanker some years previously. The port is situated in the Agersø Sound, near the Great Belt and mass of islands near Lolland.

Tugs were taken fore and aft and we were soon safely in position and lined up alongside the Chiksans®; moorings were then made fast. The ship's loading plan, agreed previously between the Master and the Chief Officer before we arrived in port, was based upon charterers' requirements stipulating the amount and grade(s) of cargo to be lifted within variable options. The plan ensured the vessel would not experience over-stressing regarding shear forces and bending moments due to incorrect weight distribution. A discussion took place between the cargo loading-superintendent, Master, Mate and available duty-officers before commencing work. Although the classification of this tanker notated her for carriage of crude oil as well as products and chemicals, for this voyage the tanker was again to load naptha across all tanks, on this occasion for delivery to Hamburg.

During such comparatively brief loading operations, sea watches were often kept, although practices vary and aboard some tankers officers worked 12-hour or even six-hourly shifts. As with discharging, the Chief Officer remained on call and monitored throughout. He or she would be readily available and build essential rest periods around less critical moments of the cargo work. The Master, meanwhile, dealt—as appropriate—with inspections from port authorities, ISM Audits, terminal inspections, ship's agents, customs, immigration, ship's chandlers and stores supplies, as well as monitoring the vessel safety and crew welfare and management from a command perspective. Loading commenced once the Chiksans® had been connected and both shore and ship notified each other that they were ready. The cargo was loaded through the same vessel cargo lines and hoses that were used for discharging in Rotterdam. The Chiksans® were bolted to the vessel's manifold, but were adjustable at the quayside to compensate for the change in freeboard of the vessel or any tidal effects.

During this loading, cargo was pumped onboard by the shore at an agreed rate of 800 tonnes per hour and distributed

Chiksan® connections between the jetty and tanker. The arms are connected to the ship's manifolds by oil-tight gaskets between the bolted connections. OCIMF recommendations supplement IMO regulations connecting these to the Chiksans® ashore designed for consistent safety standards of marine vapour recovery. On most tankers a series of reducing pieces are available ensuring that the manifold connections remain compatible with the Chiksans® (Author's Collection).

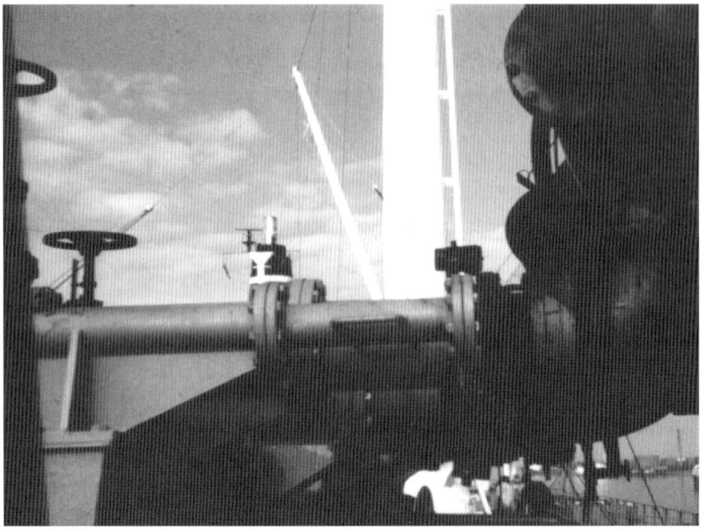

British Ensign alongside the berth in Gulfhaven showing the ship's deck crane supporting the flexible oil loading pipe. The area of bulwark below the pipe has been specially reinforced specifically for this purpose, but the pipe is raised slightly to ease strain. The placing of safety notices previously seen and the catwalk providing safe passage along the deck with red fire monitors are readily observable. Cargo pipes with breakwaters protect vulnerable pipes when the deck is sometimes awash in heavy head seas. The square boxes are ballasting vents serving the tanks, whilst jetty fire hydrant, and mooring dolphins are clearly visible (Author's Collection).

to the cargo tanks by the pipe-ring system. Segregated ballast water was simultaneously discharged. Safety remained paramount with vessel and terminal following the guidelines contained in ISGOTT (International Safety Guide for Oil Tankers and Terminals), which incorporated detailed checklists covering smoking regulations, safe access, emergency procedures, ship/shore communications, etc. All tankers are usually loaded to 98% capacity in each cargo tank, but on this occasion (for various reasons) the naptha was loaded to only 94%. The empty space left in the tank, or ullage, generally provides a built-in safety factor during 'topping-off' of the tanks at the end of loading, and allows for any cargo expansion.

The loading pattern continued over the next couple of days and proceeded according to plan, until the rate of flow was reduced to 180 tonnes per hour. This was caused by the shore-side working two cargo tanks simultaneously (one of which was close to stripping). There was an additional built-in delay to allow for the importing of additives to this particular cargo. Any delays during loading that are attributable to the vessel will normally be for the owner's account, whereas any delays attributable to the shore—which included these circumstances—are generally for the charterer to pay. They are consequently billed to the terminal account. The ship concluded loading with 29,850.56 metric tonnes—equivalent to 34,912.94 cubic metres —of density 0.8850 and temperatures around 15 °C.

Following procedures similar to those used in Rotterdam, pilot and tugs were ordered and *British Ensign* departed her berth on a draught of 10.4 metres. Before heading into open seas, the vessel was secured once more and a new passage plan from the Second Mate covered the trip to Hamburg, our designated port of discharge. For this particular passage, with its ten-hour pilotage down the River Elbe to a berth near the centre of Hamburg, the voyage plan ran to a 20-page document.

BP SHIPPING LIMITED Ref. No. MAROPS-NAV-PASSPLAN-FORM-01

bp

PASSAGE PLANNING – GENERAL VOYAGE INFORMATION

VOYAGE NO: 10/06 LOADED	FROM: GULFHAVN	TO: HAMBURG
DEPARTURE DATE: 11/11/06	DRAFTS: F = 10.50m	A = 10.50 m

Total Distance: 580 Average Speed: 14.5 Kts
Total Steaming Time: 01 day 16 hours
Requirements of STCW Section A-VIII/2.4 met

Sec. 1 GENERAL REMARKS

TO SWITCH ON AIS AND FEED IN THE NEXT PORT AND VOYAGE DETAILS
Vessel is to head for Hamburg. Vessel will be having a pilot on board from berth to Skagen and there will be a change of pilot at Grenaa.
Vessel to keep clear of the prohibited areas. All Temporary and Preliminary notices relevant and likely to be encounter on the forthcoming voyage will be penciled in on the appropriate charts for the reference of the Mariner.
Submarine Exercise Areas: Submarines frequently exercise in designated areas indicated on the charts. Notice of submarine exercises is given only in exceptional circumstances. A good lookout is to be kept for them when passing through these areas.
Risk of Collision: There is a high risk of collision, particularly in poor visibility. Apart from vessels in transit through the area in the TSS, coinciding with concentrations of fishing vessels and recreational craft.

Sec. 2 TRAFFIC

Use all means of navigational aids while navigating. Vessel should a keep a watch for small fishing crafts, which may be encountered. Use all means of navigational aids while navigating. Keep the vessel on the charted course. Keep clear from other vessels and fishing boats with a safe min CPA of 1 mile where possible. Compare gyro and magnetic compasses every 15 min Keep sharp look out for outbound vessels. Follow Masters standing & night orders.

Sec. 3 NAVIGATIONAL HAZARDS AND CAUTIONS

GPS Datum – when using the GPS to plot positions onto charts be aware of the datum being used (GPS uses WGS 84) as the datum may vary from chart to chart. Any adjustment of the GPS position should be given on the relevant chart and although in most cases the error is small, on some charts and especially some larger scale charts it may be significant.

The first page of the 20-page Passage Plan from Gulfhaven to Hamburg. Each stage of the voyage was carefully planned from the beginning of the trip to the final berth, with all courses, waypoints, meteorological and tidal information included, along with schematic diagrams giving the necessary pilotage and buoyage information (Author's Collection).

Even prior to dropping the pilot off Skagen the North Sea weather outside the Kattegat was forecast 'very rough'. It came as no surprise, once we had steadied on our course to clear Grenen (off the Swedish port of Gothenburg) and enter the Skagerrak, that we ran directly into Storm Force Ten, gusting Eleven north-westerly winds, taken directly on our starboard beam. The tanker, although fully laden, rolled 30 degrees port and 35 starboard, over an arc of 65 degrees. The five-degree difference arises from oil slopping in tanks from port to starboard, with the inevitable pause before slopping back again. Within the confines of my cabin, the motion appeared exaggerated and certainly unpredictable. Inevitably, shortly after leaving my bunk to shower and dress as a prelude to going for breakfast, I found myself being projected at speed and literally thrown across my cabin to end up in the washroom as intended. I gave my wrist a slight knock on the washbasin where I clung until common sea sense reasserted itself with the traditional rough-weather thoughts of keeping one hand for me with the other clutching firmly any conveniently stable part of the ship. To take my shower implied keeping one hand ready to reach for the usually neglected hand-rail fitted next to the shower

Photographs showing the *British Ensign* under way in Storm Force Ten winds off Jutland Bank. By the time these shots were taken, we had just altered course to the south, which placed the severe weather conditions slightly off the port quarter as opposed to directly on the beam. This made the motion perhaps less dramatic, but certainly more comfortable for all hands (Author's Collection).

controls to maintain balance and wash 'as possible' with the other. It proved a process requiring more than an element of judicious contortionism. To my surprise and joy, I was not seasick. This was probably not so much because I had 'a hardened stomach', but following some years navigating ships of varied sizes and capacities deep-sea and in the uncertainty of coastal and north-European coastal waters, what had been lost in the process was my *fear* of being seasick. I must confess the thought of being ill had crossed my mind before joining both *Anna Knutsen* and this tanker. I managed quite comfortably a light breakfast of toast, marmalade and the inevitable pot of tea—once the Master and I had managed to loosen the lashing around the six chairs at our table. In such rough weather, hot meals were not prepared, nor expected, from the galley crew. It goes without saying that no work was done by myself this particular day for my laptop and research material were comfortably settled in a corner of my settee and covered with a couple of cushions for additional safety. I did take the camera to the wheelhouse, however, managing to capture a range of shots of this event.

It was during this same storm that the ship learnt of two accidents occurring to crew members aboard other vessels. The Chief Officer of another tanker in the BP fleet, the *British Vine*, had been working on the fo'c'sle head whilst the ship was departing anchorage off Hamburg—the very port for which we were heading. A large wave unexpectedly covered completely the fo'c'sle head where he was working, the force of which washed him against the railing stanchion. He was airlifted to hospital and placed on the emergency list with critical injuries. Fortunately, he eventually recovered to be flown home for recuperation.

Seafarers aboard another non-BP ship in the same storm were not so fortunate. Three men were aboard a 74.065 s-dwt crude oil tanker that had just loaded from Scapa Flow whilst the ship was on passage in the Pentland Firth between the Orkney

Isles and the mainland, bound towards Houston in Texas. They were securing the anchor lashings and windlass equipment in preparation for sea passage across the Atlantic when a wave, estimated in excess of 20 feet, smashed over the fo'c'sle head. The force of the sea threw all three against railings with considerable force. A rescue coastguard helicopter set out from Stornoway, and the Longhope lifeboat with a doctor on board was also launched. The doctor was winched aboard the tanker, but found that two of the crew had died from their injuries whilst the third was seriously injured. He was winched to hospital by the helicopter. Storms are serious business at sea and even the coastguard duty officer stated to the BBC: 'There were westerly winds of force eight to force ten, that is somewhere around 60 mph, with very heavy seas and a high swell. The vessel, a large crude oil carrier, took the wave over the bow'. It is important to stress, however, that the weather conditions experienced on all three tankers were themselves not abnormal for the time of the year in the places where they occurred. They stand as facts that have to be accepted by all mariners without histrionics, simply as a 'part of seafaring life'. The enquiry of the Singapore authorities—the flag state of the tanker—has not yet

The small scale chart was used to plan the overall route. Marks (red on the actual chart) to the north of Denmark indicated the way-points for major alterations of course, whilst black concentric circles showed the position of the tanker at the time of photographing the entire plot (Author's Collection).

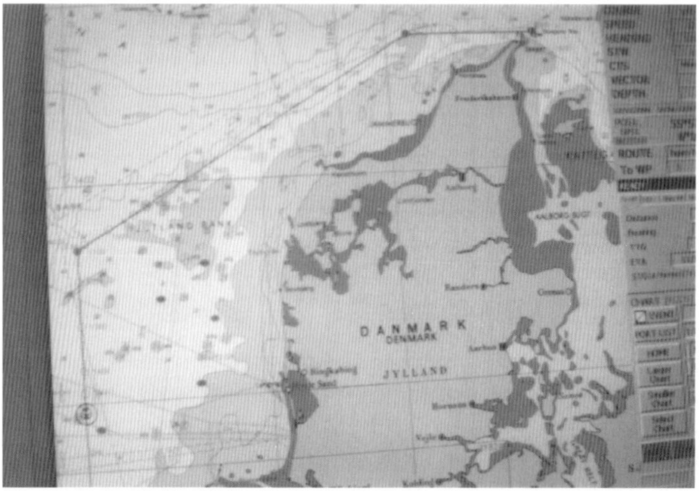

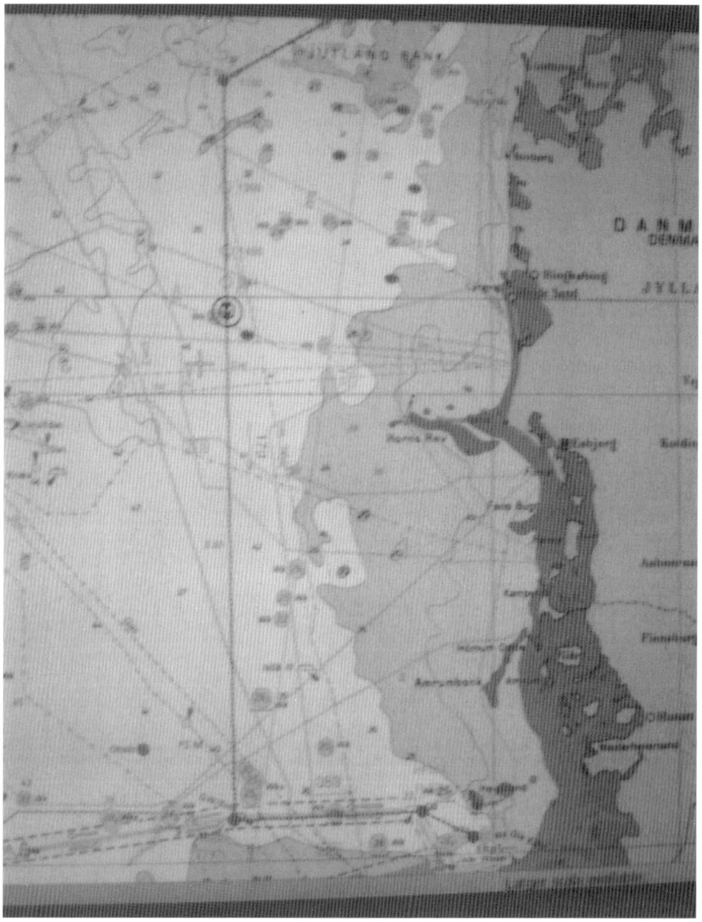

In each of the photographs, the current position of the tanker is shown by concentric circles. The forecast track to Hamburg is seen to the left or seaward side of the land mass with the major way-points for changing course leading the ship into the dredged channel and River Elbe approaches indicated by solid black dots (Author's Collection).

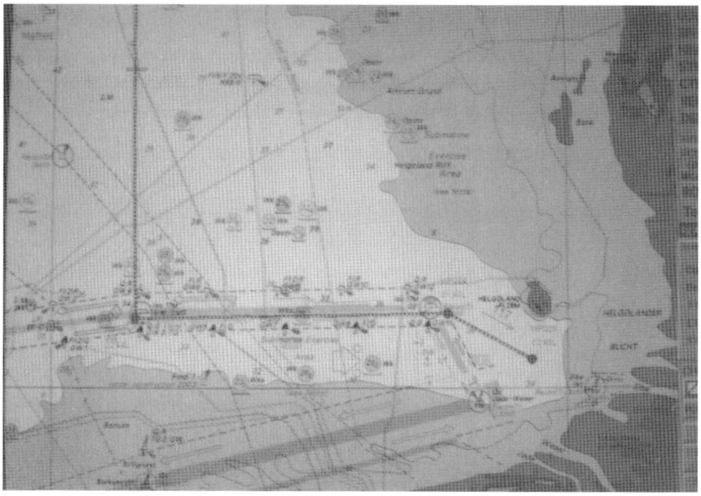

The following shot was taken whilst on passage in the River Elbe and shows the screen and controls for this particular ECDIS model. It is interesting to note the two radar PPI's (on the right-hand side) are set to different ranges and show the narrow channel in which the ship was being navigated under the advice of the pilot. These shots show the operational side of the backs of this equipment seen on page 76 (Author's Collection).

been ratified, but one of the facts they could be ascertaining might concern why the men were working in those conditions with the ship proceeding on her course for Houston, instead of these duties having been completed prior to her setting out.

The opportunity occurred, on this leg of our passage, of photographing the complete detailed passage plan from Skagen to Hamburg, witnessing the effectiveness of the Electronic Chart

Display and Information Systems (ECDIS) during an operational deep-sea trip, following the previous harbour passage out of Europoort. On this particular leg of the *British Ensign* voyage from Skagen to Hamburg, basic planning was done initially by using the smallest-scale chart to plan the overall passage, working afterwards on larger-scale charts.

The range was then decreased so that a clearer idea could be obtained not only of the current position of the ship, but the forecast track into the destination port.

The large scale 'in use' chart gave more information concerning depths of water and indications of potential navigational hazards likely to be encountered. It can be seen that by maintaining due attention to the Company's routeing plans, so keeping the tanker well offshore, the vessel was kept in deep water as much as possible and safely away from dangers of stranding.

Owing to prevailing severe weather conditions—the storm-force winds had abated little during our passage—the Master arranged for the pilot to board by helicopter, thus preventing the necessity of joining a number of other dry-cargo, container and gas carriers already established in the outer anchorage off the River Elbe. This was a straightforward operation carried out in accordance with IMO and company instructions and it passed without incident or over-much comment. Following his lowering onto the helipad, the pilot was met by our Third Officer on the catwalk and once the berthing plan and ship's 'statistics' had been discussed the vessel undertook initial stages in the lengthy passage down the Elbe towards our berth. The passage entailed taking three different river pilots. Preparations for the vessel's arrival at the discharge port had been made in advance by email communication between the charterers, owners, cargo receivers, agents and master. The discharging procedure was different from that of loading in that the vessel's own pumping equipment was used. Whilst larger tankers are often fitted with three or

BP SHIPPING LIMITED — bp — Ref. No. MAROPS-NAV-WATCH-CHECK-04

BRIDGE CHECKLIST NO.4
PREPARATION FOR ARRIVAL IN PORT

Port: HAMBURG Date: 13/11/06

	In Preparation For Arrival in Port Have the Following Been Taken Into Consideration?			
1	Arrival Port Information		YES	~~NO~~
2	Advice / Recommendations In Sailing Directions		YES	~~NO~~
3	Latest Weather Report		YES	~~NO~~
4	Tides & Current For the Port & Adjacent Areas		YES	~~NO~~
5	Tidal Diamonds & Atlas Completed		YES	NO
6	Calculation On Minimum Depth of water Available		YES	~~NO~~
7	Any restrictions On Draught, Trim, Speed, Entry Times		~~YES~~	NO
8	Charts - Pilot Station to Berth Completed		YES	~~NO~~
9	If EC Port Has Log 22 & Passage Plan Been Transmitted to Agent	N/A	~~YES~~	~~NO~~
10	Is It Necessary To Re-Arrange Cargo / Ballast		~~YES~~	NO
11	Have the Latest Navigational Messages Been Received		YES	~~NO~~
12	ETA's Sent With All Relevant Information For Port Entry		YES	~~NO~~
13	ARPA Maps On		YES	~~NO~~
14	Gyro Compass Magnetic Compass Error Obtained		YES	~~NO~~
15	Gyro Repeaters Aligned		YES	~~NO~~
	Has The Following Equipment Been Checked?			
16	Course, ~~Engine~~ & Echo Sounder Recorders Tested, paper checked, & Marked with Date		YES	~~NO~~
17	Steering gear tested		YES	~~NO~~
18	Internal Communications tested & Clocks Synchronized		YES	~~NO~~
19	Signalling Equipment Including Flags		YES	~~NO~~
20	Deck Lighting		YES	~~NO~~
21	Mooring Winches		YES	~~NO~~
22	Mooring Lines, Wires, Heaving Lines & Messengers		YES	~~NO~~
23	Pressure On Fire Main		YES	~~NO~~
24	Anchor(s) Cleared		YES	~~NO~~
25	Hydraulics / Motive Power On		YES	~~NO~~
26	Officer To Meet Pilot		YES	~~NO~~
27	Pilot Card Completed & Pilot Station To Berth Plan Completed		YES	~~NO~~
28	Stand by or second steering motor ready or in use		YES	~~NO~~
29	Manual steering in use.		YES	~~NO~~
30	Crew Advised Of Stand/by Time		YES	~~NO~~
31	Have The VHF Channels For Port Entry Been Noted		YES	~~NO~~
32	Docking Camera's on (if applicable)	N/A	~~YES~~	~~NO~~
33	Doppler log on bottom track (if applicable)	N/A	~~YES~~	~~NO~~
34	SBE EOP given (if applicable)	~~N/A~~	YES	~~NO~~
	Is the Following Information Available			
35	Whether Anchoring or Proceeding To Berth		YES	~~NO~~
36	Which Side Along Side		YES	~~NO~~
37	If Accommodation or Gangway Needed		YES	~~NO~~
38	Number and Size of Shore Connections		YES	~~NO~~
39	Cranes (or derrick's) Required		YES	~~NO~~
40	Mooring Boats or Heaving Lines		YES	~~NO~~
41	Main Engine Tested Astern		YES	~~NO~~
42	If Arriving in USA Have Requirements of CFR 164 Been Met	N/A	~~YES~~	~~NO~~
	If aplicable			
43	Bowthruster tested.?	~~N/A~~	YES	~~NO~~
44	Reporting systems messages sent.? AMVER, ~~AUSREP, JASREP~~.?	~~N/A~~	YES	~~NO~~
45	Mooring plan discussed		YES	~~NO~~
46	A/C set to recirculation	~~N/A~~	YES	~~NO~~
47	Smoking regulations posted	~~N/A~~	YES	~~NO~~

Officer: Master:

An IMO Bridge checklist for entering the port of Hamburg showing the detailed information necessary to ensure that all aspects of every duty required is not forgotten or accidentally overlooked. Meticulous preparation was essential on all occasions of port entry and departure, and the checklist provided an acceptable method of ensuring compliance. Much of this information might well come under the SMS code of some flag-States where there is some debate regarding its presentation in either digital screen viewing or as a hard copy (BP Shipping).

four large pumps, each capable of pumping at around 4,000 to 5,000 cubic metres per hour, *British Ensign* is fitted with twelve cargo pumps distributed across the port and starboard cargo wing tanks. In addition to these there is one tank-cleaning stripping pump for each cargo tank, and one serving each slop tank. There are also the separate systems incorporating one ballast pump, two fire pumps, plus an emergency fire pump.

An ECDIS display showing the *British Ensign* alongside her berth in Hamburg, where the ship is positioned towards the centre of the display and is depicted as a black concentric circle with a blaze. The windows to the right-hand side indicate an assortment of menus offering relevant navigational information (Author's Collection).

The paper 'back-up' chart of Hamburg port near the centre of the city, showing the harbour in which the tanker was berthed. The distinctive 'shape' of Hoheschaar is plainly discernable close to the centre of the main chart (Author's Collection).

Leaving *British Ensign* in Hamburg, I felt the turning of a complete circle, for my two weeks aboard that tanker had reinforced attitudes encountered during my ten days aboard *Anna Knutsen*. On this occasion, it was the sight of the Plimsoll Line, just visible below the jetty as I left the gangway, that focussed thoughts concerning my research and how things had changed since my own seagoing days. Conditions generally were considerably different then for, although safety measures were coming into their own and gradually gaining serious import, implementation of the processes examined in these three

DISCHARGE PLAN

Vessel Name : **BRITISH ENSIGN**
Voyage nmbr : **06010**

Port : **HAMBURG**
Berth :
Date : 13-Nov-06

1. ARRIVAL CONDITION

DRAFT	For'd	10.6	A	10.6	Mean	10.4
MAX BM:	19	% AT FRAME	35			
MAX SF:	16	% AT FRAME	16			

2. BALLAST CONDITION

WBT	1P	2P	3C	3P	4P	5P	6P	FPT	
QTY	235	30	40	17	40	40	40	0	
WBT	1S	2S		3S	4S	5S	6S	APT	
QTY	149	30		17	200	80	100	9	

TOTAL SEGREGATED BALLAST 1027
SLOP, IF ANY YES OIL: TOTAL: 378

3. TIDAL INFORMATION :

DATE	HIGH		LOW		HIGH		LOW	
	TIME	HEIGHT	TIME	HEIGHT	TIME	HEIGHT	TIME	HEIGHT
		SEE ATTACHED AHEET						

4. MANIFOLD/SHORE CONNECTION/LINE PLAN

IN CASE OF MULTI-GRADE CARGO HANDLING, MANIFOLD LINES PLAN MARKED CLEARLY WITH REQUIRED LINE UP/JUMPER HOSE CONNECTIONS AND PRESENTATION MANIFOLDS MUST BE ATTACHED TO THIS LOADING PLAN.

WHEN HANDLING SINGLE GRADES, IT IS SUFFICIENT TO MENTION THE IDENTIFICATION OF THE PRESENTATION MANIFOLD.

SEE PLAN

DUTY OFFICER TO PERSONALLY SUPERVISE LINES/VALVES SETTING PRIOR COMMENCEMENT OF ANY CARGO OPERATIONS.

5. CARGO TO LOAD AND STOWAGE PLAN

SEE ATTACHED SHEET

6. WATCH ARRANGEMENTS

PLEASE REFER TO NOTICE BOARD IN CCR

CHIEF OFFICER
NILESH KAWAL

MASTER
CAPT.J.S.GILL

2/O - SURESH

3/O -AJEET

3/O-AWADHUT

The Provisional Discharge Plan of the *British Ensign* covering her Naptha cargo loaded in Gulfhaven and discharged in Hamburg was contained in a six-paged document. At this early stage, the number of shore connections, which side alongside the berth and expected discharge rates/pressures would not be known and would be agreed with the pilot before coming alongside and the cargo superintendents prior to commencing discharge. All foreseeable problems would have been assessed and necessary plans made tentatively to counter the 'unknown' in the light of considerable experience loading and discharging cargoes continuously and frequently at various ports around the world (BP Shipping).

chapters proved as frustratingly tortuous, yet encouragingly certain, as Samuel Plimsoll had found when he endeavoured to introduce his measures around 150 years previously. Equally certain, the measures in each case *had* become law. For Plimsoll, as even the most shore-based 'man in the street' knows, the evidence of his success remains on the side of every international class of ship registered with a flag state. Whilst for mariners today MARPOL 73/78 (with subsequent amendments effected and proposed) and SOLAS74, along with various codes of practice and their checklists and audits, have become practical realities in the wheelhouse and in all areas aboard every member ship. In both cases, each not only continues to receive updating and revising as needs arise, but coexists with a raft of other legally enforceable measures designed specifically to ensure an ongoing attitude towards responsible implementation of safety aboard crude oil tankers. Such moves are encouraging —because safety aboard this class of ship today *is* a living entity. It seems amazing that enforcement of measures designed to ensure safety and efficiency on tankers for the good of those who operate, manage and serve as mariners rests on a history of such confused exploration and opposition. I found particularly encouraging the experiences of examining shipboard involvement in action during my voyage with BP Shipping, across most areas of maritime operations, and encountering duties performed practically with a professional attitude of awareness, which perpetuated what proved to be an atmosphere of safety and efficiency.

I felt left with a raft of unanswered questions that could simply not be dealt with aboard the two tankers. Yet paradoxically, it was discussions occurring during the two voyages themselves which had planted the seeds of these issues in my mind. I wanted to know more about such pressing points as the very few non-conforming flag states about which much had been mentioned, particularly concerning how these 'rogues' could be made to conform to the codes and conventions readily adopted by the remainder of the shipping industry. There were issues which I had discovered personally aboard *Anna Knutsen* regarding water ballast problems, as the image of those dead fish observed in the double-bottom tanks of this shuttle tanker ranged through my mind. These were just two of the other factors which I felt should at least be given an airing if my research was to be the more effective. I was filled with a resolve to seek some answers that led me, once ashore, to start a series of negotiations within the industry and embark upon a programme of extensive maritime reading.

CHAPTER FOUR

State Responsibilities and Pollution Matters

As mentioned in previous chapters, my initial and subsequent investigations aboard each tanker disclosed that the first decade of the 21st century possesses its own share of unresolved concerns regarding crude oil tankers. But, as my further research revealed, there is no doubt that these are being confronted, not just by 'lip service' but in re-assuring and positive ways. The United Nations, for example, has recognised threats to the world's oceans emanating from four sources: invasive species introduced into new environments; land-based sources of marine pollution; physical destruction of the marine habitat; and over-exploitation of living marine resources. The industry is actively seeking remedies for those areas in which it is directly involved in these concerns by addressing problems of marine and air pollution, ship safety and double-hulled tanker design.

Discussions with both captains and personnel ashore confirmed that if any action is to be successful then it is upon the registered flag states that all hopes have initially to be focussed. For these are the agencies responsible for auditing or monitoring crude oil tanker operations. This implies that the administrative and operational efficiency of these organisations assumes a vitally important role. Ever since the tanker industry shook off the sobriquet 'flags of convenience', replacing this with an 'open register' under which owners from other countries can flag their ships, fears have arisen that in some quarters this has become synonymous with substandard vessels. A very high percentage of tankers operate to equally high standards, but the continued lack of uniform enforcement of rules and regulations worldwide has opened the door to *some* substandard flag administrations. The difficulty facing responsible ship-owning communities is how to close this loophole effectively. Ship registration operates at two levels. Some lower-tier, less-committed registers have tainted the concept of open registry and raised questions about the ability of the upper level of flag-state control to prevent substandard ship-owners and operators plying their trade. It is undeniable that signatory flag states of IMO conventions are ultimate arbiters for the safety of ships registered in their country.

The chief operating officer of the Liberian Registry, writing in *Lloyd's Ship Manager* (LSM) recently focussed the problem when he said, 'Ship registries should be judged on their responsiveness, their pro-activity, their quality of service, their treatment of seafarers, their ratification and implementation of modern regulatory conventions and their safety records. Port State control and casualty records do not lie. A ship registry does not get to the top group of all major port State control jurisdictions by running a fly-by-night operation'. Speaking of the success of some of the tonnage tax regimes recently established by national flags, he said, 'It appears that the governments of these countries agree that safety and environmentally conscious convenient flags actually have it right.' He agreed, however, that some flag states 'find themselves on the wrong side of the flag of convenience argument', and his view was echoed by the president of the Marshall Islands flag-state registry. He contributed the following comment to this debate; '...there are some national registers that are substandard now. For us, one of the challenges is to continuously educate the world on the fact that the open register is not synonymous with substandard". The challenge is in introducing enforceable and appropriate legislation that will bring into line second-tier flag states continuing to oppose 'recognised norms' of the crude oil tanker industry. The International Maritime Organization (IMO) introduced in June 2006 their Voluntary Member State Audit Scheme and within three months 23 governments indicated their willingness to participate and be audited. The scheme is intended to enforce IMO standards and attain their objectives of safe, secure and efficient shipping on clean seas. It was a subtle and positive move forward. The scheme was directed at member States, but its very existence unmasks those open-register second-tier States who ignore it. How to coerce them into regulating ships under their flag becomes another matter which still remains open. As Doctor Stephen Ladyman, then a British Shipping Minister, speaking during a debate in the House of Commons on 25 January 2006 stated rather succinctly but reflecting perhaps an air of international frustration, 'Short of invading them, all we can do is engage them diplomatically.'

Environmental pollution from tankers is a top concern to virtually everyone within the industry and the 'ordinary man in the street' without, and will remain so as long as industrial and social life relies on oil. Things cannot operate in any other way. Since early experimental tankers of 150 years ago, managers and operators have worked hard at providing safe transportation for a commodity recognised as inherently dangerous. Yet, the fact that the industry has an extremely good safety record tends still to be disregarded by most people when they hear of any volume (however slight) of oil spill that might occur. Any grounding naturally and rightly attracts extensive media coverage. Recently, the Marine Coastguard Agency (MCA) was alerted to around 1,570 incidents in the UK Pollution Control Zone (UKPCZ), of which over 580 involved some form of oil or chemical discharge, of which only a *very small* number were ships of all classes. The basic reality remains that tankers today account for only a minute part of overall pollution of the seas by oil. Research by the International Association of Independent Tanker Owners (Intertanko), using figures produced by the United Nations Environmental Programme, reinforced the OCIMF view that industrial waste remains the biggest polluter of the world's oceans—at a staggering 62 per cent. Non-tanker shipping weighed in at 15%. The remaining figures comprised offshore operations (3%), refineries/terminals (1%) and other sources. By comparison, operational pollution from tankers is responsible for less than 2%—a figure that continues to fall *noticeably*. This trend continues, notwithstanding such appalling incidents such as the *Prestige* or *Sea Empress* both some years ago now. It is a moot fact that more oil enters the sea from those motorists worldwide who drain sump oil from billions of cars into town drains than from the world's collective tanker fleet.

Ongoing problems regarding air pollution face governments worldwide. The issues regarding all forms of pollution control by ships—let alone tankers—are complex and internationally inclusive. They are also difficult to unravel and explain in lay terms because intricate technical details are involved, which themselves cannot be easily simplified and explained. The fact that international agreement is required brings its own crop of difficulties in enforcement because protocols and regulations have to be universally agreed. This is a process often taking months or even years of negotiation before eventual ratification. Yet, there is an urgent need, and widespread public awareness of the need, to reduce emissions of greenhouse gases (GHG) throughout the world that are causing catastrophically damaging and irreversible effects, particularly from the major source of millions of worldwide industrial sites. These latter sources of course pollute also the world's oceans. With the lack of major new oil finds over the last fifteen years, non-OPEC oil supply is likely to grow slowly. Unless cheap alternative sources of energy can be discovered, soon OPEC's role and strength will increase in the future world oil markets. The world needs to assess its consumption of fossil-based fuels and to seek alternatives, where these are viable, with positive steps taken to control emissions from the world's estimated one billion cars by 2020 and 20,000 jet-planes. Steps were taken as long ago as 1990 that resulted in cleaner car fuels and today many responsible motorists worldwide use unleaded petrol. Many countries are running cars on alternative fuels resulting from developments in fuel constitution, additives and biological products. The progress, however, is not keeping pace with the damage done *now* to the world's Arctic and Antarctic regions. Media coverage extending over many months has focussed graphically on effects of melting at the Arctic ice cap, with worrying footage illustrating the damage being created.

Seen in proportion, the approximately 10,000 tankers of all classes remain a modestly inoffensive offender—but an offender nevertheless. A Bulk Liquids and Gas (BLG) sub-committee was set up by IMO's Marine Environment Protection Committee (MEPC) in late 2006, which continues to develop a range of measures covering reduction of ship carbon dioxide (CO_2) emissions. Also included are recommendations and criteria relevant to exhaust gas sulphur oxide (SO_x) cleaning systems, wash-water discharges, and further implementation of nitrogen oxide (NO_x) emissions. All of these matters are consolidated under amended MARPOL 73/78 Annex VI Protocols and continue to be revised and implemented so that the industry can do, and be seen to do, the maximum possible in cleaning up operating and other practices aboard all ships. Indeed, evidence of the strenuous efforts in force for combating air pollution by gas emission from ships' exhausts was encountered aboard *Anna Knutsen*. IMO's Marine Environmental Protection Committee (MEPC) has been working for some years now urging and refining acceptance of regulations designed specifically to limit and reduce as much as possible the GHG polluting the earth's atmosphere. A standard form of compliance certification has been introduced, facilitating enforcement across all ships, including tankers, of all nations by flag-state authorities. Their concern is expressed by other responsible agencies, including Intertanko who work within a 'round table' consortium of Intercargo, the International Chamber of Shipping (ICS) and the Baltic and International Maritime Council (BIMCO) which is an association of important ship owners. Unhampered by restrictive boundaries of collective discussion, Intertanko some years ago initiated positive action recommending their members—who influence a considerable proportion of the world's ocean-going tonnage—to abandon residual fuels for ships' bunkers, and switch to distillate fuels such as marine diesel oil (MDO) in efforts to reduce NO_x emissions from ships' engines. Residual fuel is that remaining after refining crude oil by removing higher-grade oils, and is used for fuelling marine engines during ocean passages. MDO is generally one of the 'higher grades' and contains less sulphur, with a 'knock-on' reduction in other noxious gases. Already, IMO has set provisional dates for the capping of sulphur oxide emissions from ships, a decision that has been helped by the introduction of new marine diesel engines setting tighter standards of nitrogen oxide emissions, making them increasingly environmentally friendly. One problem the industry has to overcome is that of attracting support to carry the costs involved. Providing bunkers is the most expensive single cost of running a large ship, working out around 55% of the voyage costs for VLCCs. Because it is more expensive, diesel is normally used only during docking, harbour passages or trips in restricted waters when greater control is required over the ship, necessitating frequent use of the engines and requiring more stopping and starting movements. Intertanko's suggestion was acclaimed by the shipping industry as bold and worthy of serious consideration. That mouthpiece of international maritime affairs, *Fairplay* shipping magazine, commented: 'This is as obvious as it is radical, but it is a brave decision nevertheless. In the past it has been okay to think radical thoughts but not to express them. Now the cat is out of the bag and Intertanko is being applauded for its boldness'. Suggestions for implementation include use of a fixed oxygen analyser for the vapour manifold and effective means of transferring ashore volatile organic compounds (VOCs) during loading.

Other advances being made by the industry to cut fuel emissions include use of shore power supply connections in place of the ship's main engines to run generators or, as it is referred to, 'cold ironing' which enables the engines and generators to be switched off. This idea is encouraged by increasing numbers of ports working towards providing the necessary facilities.

A major United Nations concern being dealt with is the loading, transporting and discharging of ballast water by tankers. The water enters a *segregated* ballast system to increase ship stability, bringing the ship down to light draught mark levels submerging bulbous bow, rudder and propeller. This is then pumped out on arrival at the next port whilst loading another cargo. As long ago as February 2004, IMO adopted the International Convention for the Control and Management of Ships' Ballast Water and Sediments. The 'Ballast Water Management Convention' (BWMC) required all ships to implement a ballast and sediments plan for flag-state inspection following an awareness documentary film launched in March 2006 entitled *Invaders from the Sea*. Vela International Shipping, BP Shipping, Wallenius-Alfa Laval Consortium sponsored the production—with support from 'GloBallast pilot countries' incorporating China, Iran, India, Ukraine, South Africa and Brazil. The film was distributed through the United Nations in developing countries, and elsewhere using the resources of BBC worldwide television. This highlighted the manner in which harmful organisms are transported across the world in the ballast water of all ships—but especially tankers—creating biological, economic and ecological havoc. Preventative measures were introduced controlling the estimated 3 to 10 billion tonnes of ballast water used annually by ships containing a variety of wildlife species released into non-native environments. The film depicted three organisms and showed evidence of their harmful effects upon release: North American comb jelly transported into the Black and Azov seas during the 1990s, contributing to the death of a local fish industry in the Caspian Sea; golden mussel carried from Asian rivers and creeks to Brazil and upriver to Argentina that clogged up the water intake pipes of hydroelectric power stations and affected fish stocks; in the third portrayal, transporting toxic algae which caused oxygen depletion along the South African coastline, fouling beaches, affecting tourism, but more dangerously, contaminating shellfish to an extent that, without urgent treatment to a patient, paralysis and death could have resulted. Since this film's release an estimated 73% of species imported into Australian waters came into their seas on the hulls of ships of all classes and not through ballast-water exchanges.

Lloyd's Ship Manager magazine pointed to the existence of ten plants, animals and microbes carried around the world attached to the hulls of all classes of ship and in their ballast water, which are potentially dangerous to any new environments into which they could be pumped. Positive action is being taken seriously by the industry. All new builds delivered after 2009, for example, require a system fitted capable of treating or killing a host of aquatic organisms—and by 2014, all ships will need an onboard ballast-water treatment-plant. If any problems are presented at all, these revolve around availability of the essential treatment technology to combat the problem. One of these was situated in Japan, a second in Norway, and the third at Key West in Florida. More centres are needed if viable legislation is to result, particularly as (currently) testing operations take several weeks. Ballast-water transfers have become a major talking-point and an IMO meeting in Conference October 2006, adopted guidelines implementing the 2004 Ballast Water Management Convention (BWMC).

Even before the turn of the century, Intertanko had expressed fears concerning unilateral legislation introduced by a number of independent American States particularly, that were restricted to *regional* activity. The laws had been introduced without international or federal agreement and created dangerous precedents that could easily open the floodgates for other regions world-wide to enact similar regulations. In 2000, Intertanko won a lengthy battle in the United States Supreme Court preventing the State of Washington from enacting local legislation. *Fairplay* focussed on a further incidence of local enactments when they highlighted action by the State of California which passed a Coastal Ecosystems Protection Act banning ballast-water discharges from commercial shipping. The magazine expressed fears that it might be only a matter of time before other States follow suit, although they forecast a considerable battle before California's Act became federal law.

IMO have been active also in implementing resolutions revising standards covering treatment of sewage, by instituting a plan confronting ongoing issues of port reception facilities. Notwithstanding efforts in this area, discharging many waste products ashore remains a very real problem in some areas of the world. Reports indicate some ports charge expensive fees for using their facilities and raise technical issues almost bordering on excuses along the lines, 'Is the oil you wish to land the right type of oil for our facilities?' Evidence exists that some ports insist on rigid separation of landed waste by the crews of tankers—ever ready to cooperate—who find that segregated discharged material, instead of being recycled, is placed into one common landfill site. It would seem that some incompatibility exists through the lack of an international discharge policy, perhaps caused by inadequate governmental funding for resource facilities. Intertanko have established for some years now the Industrial Port Facility Forum that was supported by both the EU and IMO to act as a positive way forward. Through a common meeting-point for discussion, information and guidance are offered, focussing thoughts and resources towards achieving a solution. Support received from a number of responsible governments shows promise of developing into constructive action. The idea sustaining Intertanko's philosophy includes encouraging the policing of those ports authorities responsible—not from a view so much of catching the culprits (although this is important) but more to 'naming and shaming', which might encourage the irresponsible into wanting their names removed from such a list. The action would be positive by supporting those already conforming. There is little doubt the tanker industry is a lone voice possessing little 'clout', so perhaps the answer resides in closer cooperation with environmental agencies, with responsible port authorities showing the way to flag states.

CHAPTER FIVE

Tanker Construction and Safety

Today, all crude oil tankers in regular service are double-hulled and sided, but the acclaimed ships of twenty or so years ago have, in the eyes of some authorities, not lived up to all expectations. The ships *are* fundamentally safe, which is just as well seeing that both the industry and the world have to live with them. The question in the early days revolved around the use of high-tensile steel (HTS) which has been commonplace in the hull plating and structural support members of VLCCs since the 1970s. Some Japanese practices of HTS treatment during rolling where the thermal mechanically controlled process (TMCP) produces finer degrees of plate thickness tolerance has caused concerns because some Japanese-built ships had as much as 70% of their steel-weight in this lighter-gauge HTS. Evidence from the last twenty years has shown that problems arise when too great a percentage of high-tensile steel is used in the construction of large tankers. Some designers believe the principal commercial advantages of HTS, reduced hull steel-weight and easier welding, are offset by the lower corrosion safety factor, and the shorter fatigue life of this type of steel. In contrast, it seems that the use of thicker, conventional mild steel leads to reduced stress levels and less time on maintenance and steel renewal due to corrosion. The consensus of opinion is that high levels of HTS *can* be used in the construction of large ships, providing accurate assessment is made of structural design details and fatigue life. In recent years the average percentage of HTS in VLCC new-buildings has dropped, in many cases to below 40%. The subject of HTS and the Japanese TMCP has fortunately been addressed but memories linger of the initial furore this created in the industry.

Primary protection of tankers lies in the correct application of adequate coatings to segregated water ballast tanks. It is probably the easiest operating factor of crude oil tanker hull integrity to which the non-specialists can relate, because car owners are well aware of corrosive effects to their vehicles and the damaging results that can occur when this is untreated. As it was observed with each of the BP Shipping and Knutsen OAS tankers, the double bottom and double side spaces of most crude oil tankers are fitted to carry ballast water. This is an ideal arrangement because the system has its own pumps and piping lines. Many tankers have two sets of ballasting pumps driven by electric motors provided for ballasting/de-ballasting, whilst most have ballast-tank capacity exceeding that required by the rules to reduce hull stresses in the ballast condition. This improves cargo loading and the integrity of the ship's structure. Virtually all ballast tanks have coats of light-coloured, tar-free, epoxy coatings to minimise corrosion and facilitate inspection and maintenance. The double-bottom areas aboard a VLCC are between 2½ and 3 metres depth with double side spaces of similar width facilitating inspections. The light colouring makes it easier to identify possible cracks and flaws than the heavy dull colours of yesteryear. The latter are important points, as a marine superintendent with a large London-based shipping company was quick to confirm: 'Dark coatings make leakages from small defects in welds/parent material, pinholes, hairline fractures, that much more difficult to locate, and make inspections slower with that much more time spent in tanks.' Although hull structural analysis, including fatigue assessment, is carried out by ship classification societies, further improvements are required to class rules addressing detailed design and fatigue assessment. Gas detectors are installed in the ballast tanks spaces of many tankers with facilities for equipping them with clean air detection systems and emergency inert gas connections.

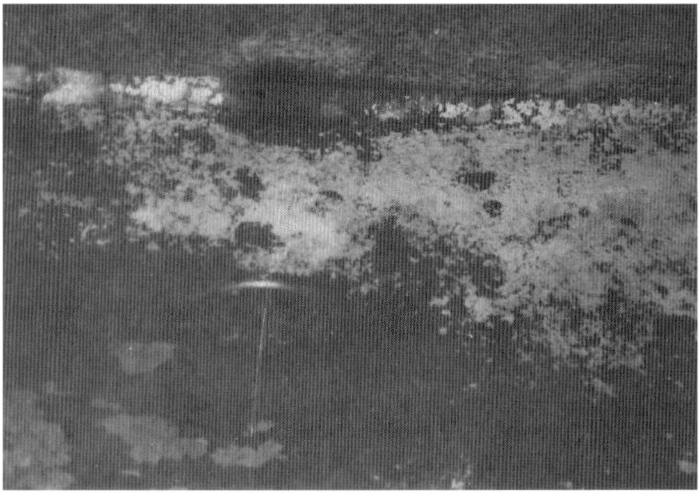

During regular routine inspections of water ballast tanks the kind of potential defects or flaws looked for as being necessary for immediate treatment are small holes that might have been left during coatings which could easily lead to rusting (Jotun Paints, Europe Ltd.).

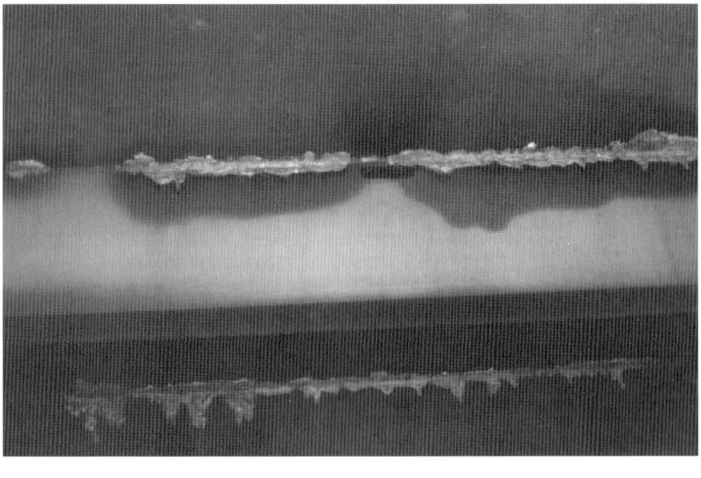

Marine growths that occur over a period of years at the corners of ballast tanks need only to 'have an eye kept of them' during inspections to see that they do not increase proportionally. If this occurs, then remedial treatment would be taken (Author's Collection).

Some classification societies and other interested professional organisations hold concerns that chlorine-based paints might increase rather than diminish corrosion rates. The Norwegian Classification Society, following their study on the effects of ozone-based ballast-water systems on tank structure, concluded the threshold for safe ozone dosage was relatively low: 'Most systems use some form of oxidation but if you increase the oxidation process you increase the corrosion rate. Ozone is an excellent biocide and is very efficient, but unfortunately such are the effects on steel you can actually see corrosion taking place in front of your eyes.' Seen alongside the IMO ballast-water tank coating performance standards which came into force during 2008, examinations of greater depth were possible into the nature of ballast-tank coatings. Classification societies continue studying the question of structural fatigue, while groups such as the Tanker Structure Co-operative Forum (TSCF)—formed in 1982—have investigated material selection and identified the critical areas relating to structural integrity and corrosion.

In addition to ballast-tank difficulties, cargo-tank corrosion was identified early in the service of some double-hulled crude oil tankers. First signs appeared in the under-deck plating of uncoated cargo tanks to depths of 3-4 mm—very similar to that experienced in single-hulled vessels—proving the problem was not a new one to the industry. That this had happened so quickly, within two to three years, into the life of the new constructions caused considerable consternation. Generally, in single-hulled tankers evidence was not detected until well into the life of the ship—perhaps as late as around her third special five-year survey, or fifteen to eighteen years into service. The cause was in some respects quite simple. In the single-hulled VLCC, there was perhaps 20 mm or so thickness of shell plating next to the cooler seawater that kept down the cargo temperature to a level that discouraged marine growths. The width of a double-hulled vessel acts as insulation of the cargo tank from the cooler sea, leaving a moist warm internal tank, with an abundance of food in the form of steel, particularly tempting to marine growths. As long ago as April 2000, the industry (Intertanko) produced guidelines: *Corrosion Onboard Crude Oil Tankers—Cargo Tank Corrosion Awareness Guide* and, after close collaboration with the Tanker Structure Co-operative Forum (TSCF) and classification societies, recommendations were offered for diagnostic approaches in a later report suggesting solutions for existing tankers and new-builds. For the former, coating of the tank should follow remedial repairs whilst, for the latter, partial coatings should be applied as appropriate to the specific ship and tanks. Often these suggestions necessitated reviews of current practices. For instance, welding might well solve the problem of corrosion repair in existing cargo tanks, but could damage ballast tank coatings on the other side of the plates, which in itself would necessitate their coating. It led, in most tankers, to cargo tanks having a protective coating one metre from the tank bottoms, and similarly a one-metre coating down from the deck-heads, modified with tar epoxy to minimise damage caused by such microbial corrosion. Whilst on the subject of safety in cargo tanks, all new tankers are fitted with gauging and alarm systems in the cargo pump room and the action of switching on lighting activates a ventilation system. There are two alarms, the first activating when hydrocarbon concentrations in the pump room reach 10% of the lower explosive limit (LEL), and the second at 30% LEL.

External protection of the hull remains important in ship operation. The hull of a crude oil tanker has to be protected against two dangers: fouling by marine growths and corrosion. When treating these it is necessary to exercise care, ensuring that coatings applied as anti-fouling do not conflict with anti-corrosives. The problem is not a new one and for years specialist paint manufacturers have spent resources studying these two specific difficulties. Their findings have led to the design and application of special coatings to underwater areas of crude oil tankers. The problems are particularly emphasised with VLCCs whose deep slow-moving hull provides an ideal breeding-ground for all manner of 'maritime nasties'. The same areas of oil storage vessels (FPSOs)—themselves V/ULCCs of course—prove equally susceptible to Acorn and Gooseneck barnacles, *Entomorpha* and *Ectocarpus* growths (amongst others) together with the microorganism known as 'good old-fashioned' slime. Traditional methods of hull protection against fouling used toxic paints possessing tributyl tin oxides (TBTs) which were applied over the anti-corrosive coatings. Marine growths fed on these, became poisoned and dropped off into the sea. Unfortunately, the tin in the anti-fouling, that proved so protective of the hull, also poisoned the environment, resulting in introduction of the IMO Control of Harmful Anti-Fouling Systems on Ships Convention that banned their use from 1 January 2008. Maintaining hull integrity and environmental protection has meant treating the shell plating from bilge keel to boot topping using a number of layers of self-polishing coal-tar epoxide resin-based paint coatings, which have worked well with other protective agencies applied to the hull and proved highly resistant to water and chemical interactions. The painting process was planned over the five-year dry-docking period so that as one layer became gradually consumed another one was revealed. A problem remains with new anti-corrosion and fouling coatings that have replaced TBTs. These are mainly either zinc- or copper-based biocidal coatings that are not so effective and lead to the necessity of additional protection. This has led to a further difficulty. The replacement raw materials zinc and copper are far more expensive than tin and are subject to increasing costs to the suppliers—which inevitably have to be passed on to the shipowner. Even alternatives such as aluminium and iron ore are facing increasing costs, and considerable debates seem to have arisen within the industry, which often became quite heated as shipowners jockey for a beneficial financial position with some paint manufacturers.

The debate about twin-engine tankers is also ongoing. The two engines fitted to modern Stena tankers do not represent the norm for most crude oil tankers: they are exceptional features for exceptional tankers. The argument for twin-engine tankers is not a new one and is almost as old as the tanker itself. Whilst fittings to the Stena ships are required for greater manoeuvrability, suiting these particular hull designs, their fitting

Examples of the type of marine growths in the form of goose-neck barnacles and slime which need to be removed during periodic surveys as they impede the progress of the tanker through the water (Jotun Paint, Europe Ltd.).

The world's largest tanker *Jahre Viking* (now a FPSO called *Knock Nevis*) passing through the Suez Canal shows the effectiveness of a planned cycle of hull maintenance with successive layers of anti-fouling/corrosive paint consumed by the passage of the ship through the water (Jotun Paints, Europe Ltd.).

to all modern crude oil tankers, constructed to traditional designs, has not been considered necessary by the wider industry. Generally, a single propeller of the type fitted to most tankers has a right-turning action—in a clockwise direction, causing the ship's head to swing to port owing to propeller thrust. This has a number of practical considerations. A captain needs to place the ship precisely where he or she wants it to go, often without tugs, and frequently in adverse crosswinds and tides. In these circumstances the propeller thrust of a single screw is a considerable asset. In an emergency, for example, it is sometimes necessary to make a complete 360° round turn, perhaps for collision avoidance purposes. With a right-handed revolving screw, the turning-circle is tighter turning to port than to starboard and helps achieve a more controlled turn. Propeller thrust is also useful when approaching an anchorage or during a pilotage berthing operation. Some professional master mariners argue that some large tankers fitted with two engines may lose some of these advantages, especially at the slow speeds often required for these manoeuvres, whilst others disagree. There is also the additional cost of fitting two engines. Additionally, the propulsion systems of modern tankers are very powerful and utterly reliable. Propulsion of a 290,000 s-dwt VLCC, for example, may consist of a fixed-pitch propeller driven by a slow-speed diesel engine developing 30,000 bhp at 75 rpm to provide a ship service speed of 15 knots. Normally, three-diesel generator sets provide electrical power aboard modern tankers of the VLCC class, while two marine boilers and an exhaust gas economiser meet steam requirements. The vessel also has a software package monitoring and controlling machinery performance, and offers an enhanced diagnostic capability. Each of these separate items makes major contributions towards safety and efficiency.

The twin rudders and propellers fitted to the 312,000 s-dwt V-Type tankers *Stena Vision* and *Stena Victory* designed to suit a unique hull shape which has made revolutionary advances in modern supertanker design (Stena Bulk Shipping).

CHAPTER SIX

Human Concerns

The crews aboard both the BP and Knutsen tankers felt valued by their employers and virtually all expressed satisfaction with the seafaring way of life. 'Nothing succeeds like success', we are told, and certainly the crews interviewed felt they had made correct decisions when joining their respective merchant navies initially and were optimistic about the future. Indeed, most were sufficiently ambitious in their desires to proceed along clearly determined career paths leading to senior positions afloat and ashore.

For many years now fears have been expressed in the United Kingdom, reflecting disquiet experienced in countries worldwide as maritime nations seek solutions to problems in recruiting future officers from a younger generation seemingly reluctant to seek seagoing careers. The world has watched a steady decline in the number of cadets and trainees, *since the 1980s* when cadet recruitment for deck and engineering officer cadets in the UK was stopped. In Britain since that date, few editions of Nautilus UK, *The Telegraph*, the officer union's magazine, have failed to contain at least one leading article on these subjects. They have made successive recommendations to successive governments urging a continuum in numbers and quality of navigating and engineering officer cadets essential for safeguarding future officer numbers and efficiency. Their fears have been echoed by other authoritative sources. *Lloyds Ship Manager*, for example, as long ago as 1997, in an article entitled 'Bitten by the Officer Gap' commented: 'Even though efforts have been made recently to increase recruitment of cadets in the UK and numbers have increased slightly, they are still falling well short of the figure needed to maintain even the present levels of British officers.' The situation has not improved significantly.

Nautilus UK has also exercised fears on retaining seafarers internationally once they have been recruited, with concerns expressed regarding not only enticing suitable youngsters away from other 'more alluring' professions, but retention of crews once they were serving at sea. A series of varied articles address the problems: fatigue levels of officers and crew due to the reduction in manning scales, pay and conditions of service, responsibility of officers for ship pollution offences and the lowering of standards of some foreign officers serving on British ships. The *Telegraph*—and journals with a maritime theme—do not merely 'beat a drum', for the points addressed are matters of real concern directly affecting the safety and efficiency of all ships, including tankers of every trade, size and flag.

It was in November 2006 that the *Telegraph*, in a major pull-out supplement, focussed concerns about the industry's 'looming skill shortage', indicating potential involvement of marine insurance brokers. They reported 'growing concern among marine insurers that the shipping industry's failure to recruit and retain quality officers could have a detrimental effect on risk management, leading to more losses and ultimately forcing up insurance premiums.' Certainly, the majority of tanker accidents, and incidents resulting in 'near misses', are directly attributable to human error. The magazine advised of reports from BIMCO predicting by 2015, 'a shortfall of some 27,000 officers, or 6% of the total workforce,' whilst the International Shipping Federation (ISF) advised: 'the current worldwide officer shortfall at 10,000... (when)...the worldwide demand for qualified officers is 476,000.' The *Telegraph* quoted increasing concerns and recommendations from the chairman of a leading risk management and insurance company: 'Shipping companies must review their strategies for recruitment, training and retention before a bad situation becomes a full-blown crisis.' Crew quality had been assessed by the insurance industry during their three-day 2007 international conference in Japan gathering 360 marine underwriters from 41 different national member associations. The culprits are not the leading international shipowners, who foresee crises developing, recruit quality crews across all levels and offer excellent facilities to encourage training and retention. *Tanker Operator* magazine, reinforcing the insurance industry's concerns, wrote recently of the reality of crewing. IMO recognised many of the concerns at a recent conference, when the MSC agreed to a comprehensive review of the STCW Code and Convention to bring this in line with new challenges facing the industry in the later stages of this decade, and the foreseeable future. The responsible sub-committee were instructed to define issues necessary for review and, working as necessary with the NAV sub-committee, review the safe manning levels aboard ships.

On a more optimistic note, there have been some encouraging signs during 2008/9 of a reawakening of interest on the part of youngsters, with increased numbers of cadets presenting themselves for officer training, but the numbers remain woefully inadequate in the light of current officer needs throughout the maritime industry and many associated companies ashore who look to experienced officers for their senior personnel.

Another disturbing aspect relating to employment of ships' officers concerns crew competence. The January 2006 *Telegraph* mentioned a containership detained in an American port after

US Coastguard officials discovered that five junior officers were not holding flag-state endorsements to their certificates of competency. In June of the same year, *Fairplay* ran a special report highlighting concerns arising from the deterioration of standards in professional examinations for Class 1, 2 and 3 certificates of competency, allegedly owing to 'the bar being dropped for examination pass-marks'. A number of practical incidents were related of practices at sea showing unbelievable incompetence, reinforcing laments heard from numerous Masters over the *past few decades* concerning junior mates' reluctance to 'look out of the wheelhouse windows occasionally and actually *see* what is going on'—rather than relying totally on electronic information from radar and instruments for information essential for position-fixing. Equally disturbing is the increased number of reports in recent issues of the *Telegraph* covering fraudulent practices on the part of some nationals trying to obtain illegally deck and engineering certificates of competency. Courts in varying countries administer justice, with imposed sentences ranging from large fines and expenses to recommendations for the guilty offender to serve two hundred hours' community service.

A vast range of up-to-date officer and crew training manuals were found aboard both tankers. This incorporated video- and computer-based interactive programs covering a range of safety and ongoing training in navigation and seamanship, as well as covering requirements for engineering staff. The quality of all of these packages was superb. The material had clearly been well thought through and was available for any mariner to use during officer-led bad weather training sessions and off-duty evening personal training for cadets and those interested in gaining advancement within their chosen areas.

This high standard of material has been reflected in a range of shore-based training. Experiences gained during simulator

The navigating officer of yesteryear identifies a potential target of navigational interest on the radar and confirms by visual lookout with binoculars in a reaction that is almost instinctive. Even in today's era of high technology a combination of experience and observation can provide more information regarding the state of the sea and the way the ship is riding the waves than can impersonal equipment (BP Shipping).

exercises ashore in the 1990s led to the enhancement of simulators improving officer training. *Tanker Operator* reported recently on a new navigation training simulator for ship-handling and bridge-operation opened in Northrop Grumman Corporation of America's first Sperry Marine training centre in Hamburg. The training mimics a ship's bridge with a 4.2-metre wide 120° panoramic screen. The simulator has replication of bridge controls and integrated bridge systems including ECDIS, autopilot, heading and speed controls, manual or autopilot steering, heading and speed indicators. The magazine reported also on Kelvin-Hughes' range of 'S-Band SharpEye TM' radars that were acclaimed as 'the most revolutionary innovation in the marine navigation market since the introduction of commercial radar in the 1940s'. As Kelvin-Hughes rightly assert, assessing radar technological advances over the preceding forty years, 'There have been notable improvements which have helped to produce a clearer radar picture and add valuable new tools to help the navigator. ARPA, motion stabilisation, image orientation options, interference rejection, high-resolution daylight viewing colour displays, electronic chart overlays and scan to scan correlation have all had significant impact on the way commercial marine navigation works'. Amongst the features making SharpEye radar equipment different was the elimination of the magnetron and high-voltage modulators enabling digital detection techniques 'normally only found in multi-million dollar systems to be available in commercial marine radars'. The system detects targets in sea clutter (the weakness of most radar systems of yesteryear, to the frustration of generations of navigating officers) using Doppler to detect a target's velocity and add additional refinements. This sophisticated radar is integrated into the world's first widescreen bridge using KH's MantaDigital TM common core processors. The chart radar complies adequately with the new IMO standards implemented in 2009. The MantaDigital range is extended by Kelvin-Hughes with their S-VDR voyage data recorder.

The Marine and Coastguard Agency, in a laconic introduction to their booklet *Personal Survival at Sea*, issued to every seafarer and found aboard all UK merchant ships, asserted 'no one is a survivor until rescued'. In the *Titanic* disaster, 1,489 persons were in water at 0°C for just under two hours and none survived. Events during the Second World War proved the majority of survivors from sunken ships of both the Royal and merchant navies died of either hypothermia or drowning. In calm water at 5°C a casually dressed person has only a 50%

For many years now there has been simulator training consistent with STCW requirements, which is very much 'hands-on' such as this bridge and wheelhouse trainer. Here, 'own ship' can be navigated in the approaches to Sydney Inner Harbour in varying traffic conditions during day or night passages using equipment found on the bridge of any selected class of ship (Transas Marine).

Warsash Maritime Academy in Southampton has for thirty years used practical ship models of very large vessels for experienced senior officer and pilot training where additional ship-handling skills learnt in the class-room can be practised. The lake is sufficiently large for practising manoeuvres involving potential collisions and bringing a large ship alongside (George Hammond).

Open viewing radars have been in existence now for many years aboard all classes of vessel. The obvious advantages are that more than one person may view the display simultaneously which assists discussion of potential collision or navigational data and as well as proving invaluable for training purposes (Racal-Decca Marine).

chance of survival, extended by wearing a lifejacket, but even more where the person is wearing an immersion suit. Wearing the former has been compulsory since the *Titanic* enquiry, and now provision of the latter for each crewmember aboard cargo ships and bulk carriers is compulsory under the provisions of SOLAS Chapter III, Regulation 32, which became enforceable in 2006. Wearing an immersion suit implies there could be a reduction in loss of body heat—although this depends upon whether the thickness and quality meets SOLAS standards. Even in enclosed lifeboats in temperate waters, as *Tanker Operator* pointed out recently, 'Modern enclosed lifeboats provide excellent protection but they can get cold and in high latitudes which is life threatening, wearing an immersion suit will mean the difference between comparative comfort and teeth chattering misery'. In southern latitudes where warmer weather may be experienced, the wearing of immersion suits in totally enclosed lifeboats has to be treated with caution for there have been recorded instances of people overheating with dehydration occurring.

The suits are not in themselves purely flotation devices so, unless fitted with an internal flotation device of the type found in helicopters, the mariner needs a lifejacket. The sales director of a commercial firm providing personal protective equipment (PPE) spoke to *Safety at Sea International* expressing a warning held by a number of international manufacturing organisations, when he stated, 'If, for instance, air collects in the knee area of an immersion suit, it may be more difficult to successfully self-right the wearer. We test our products for compatibility with immersion suits, but not all manufacturers do so.' To comply with SOLAS, the suit has to support the wearer's head when floating face-up, which keeps the wearer's mouth clear of the water enabling him or her to breathe comfortably in all sea conditions. Some suits have a foam buoyancy pillow fulfilling SOLAS requirements.

Amongst risks associated with seafaring that until the autumn of 2008 rarely became public knowledge are piracy and armed robbery. This was brought home forcibly to the world through the medium of our television screens when the ULCC *Sirius Star* was hijacked in November 2008. The tanker, owned by a major shipping international, was on passage from Saudi Arabia to the United States by way of the Cape of Good Hope when it was captured by Somali pirates. At the time, it was 450 nautical miles (830 km) south east of Kenya with

Compulsory pre-sea training courses involve introductory teaching in the use of life-saving gear and personal survival equipment. Here trainees at sea school practise 'righting procedures' with a life-raft in the safety of the swimming pool before trying the ventures out of doors (Athel Line).

Seafarers practice drills out-doors with an inflated life-raft, including pre-boarding procedures, whilst a trainee equipped in a modern life preserving fitted survival suit proves the efficacy of the gear. The suit comes complete with suitable foot-ware and is designed to be devoid of air pockets that could potentially result in impaired buoyancy. Note also the supported neck and face hood protecting the mouth and helping retain warmth. In these drills, the sea is calm and devoid of swell–often the reality of the conditions where this vital equipment might be required in earnest are not so favourable (*Fairplay* Shipping magazine).

Conforming to IMO Regulations all seafarers are required to attend a fire-fighting course ashore prior to proceeding to sea and then at intervals during their service. Realistic practical fire-fighting training is followed by trainees at a sea school which is often supervised by local fire brigade officers who support lecturing staff. A range of close up and distance fires are tackled with temperatures often well in excess of 200°C (Athel Line and *Fairplay* Shipping magazine).

a full load of crude oil. It was manned by one of the mixed-nationality 25 crew-members mentioned previously, from Saudi Arabia, Great Britain (the chief engineer and second officer), Philippines, Croatia and Poland. The ship at 330 metres and of 320,000 s-dwt was the largest vessel captured by piracy which is why it attracted considerable attention from the world's media for a few days. That it was a fully laden oil tanker with two million barrels of crude oil on board added piquancy in the eyes of the general public, especially when enthusiastic journalists erroneously converted this figure into billions of gallons/litres.

It is quite obvious that the modern pirate no longer fits the storybook stereotype, but is generally a class-member of agile and highly mobile young men who make a seemingly lucrative career terrorising the crews of ships and often stealing the

The VLCC *Sirius Star* hit the headlines when it was hijacked by pirates in 2008 projecting into the public domain a problem that had been confronting the maritime world for many years. This was the most ambitious project undertaken by piracy as previously the many vessels involved had been of smaller capacity tonnage (U. S. Navy and W. S. Stevens).

ship itself complete with cargo sometimes for onward re-selling. Certainly, in the face of considerable opposition from the Saudi government, the owners of *Sirius Star* negotiated a ransom from $25 million dollar to allegedly one of $12 million soon after the ship was taken. It is a measure of the lucrative nature of this illegal business. The tanker was eventually released in January 2009 following negotiations and payment of an alleged £2m ransom—which still represents a tidy sum of money.

Earlier, in August the tug/anchor handling vessel *Yenenogoa Ocean* was seized by pirates off the Horn of Africa and was subsequently converted into a mother ship for the pirates enabling them to widen their sphere of operations. Perhaps it was pirates from this same vessel that attacked *Sirius Star*, because they clearly spread their nets widely. Later in April 2009, the 17,000 grt all-American-manned container ship *Maersk Alabama,* whilst some 300 miles from Somalia, was hijacked. The master Captain Richard Phillips of Vermont offered himself as hostage to protect both his twenty-man crew and vessel. He was released after being held in a lifeboat for five days when forces of the American Navy rescued him and, in the process, killed three of the pirates. Moller-Maersk has subsequently restricted entry of their vessels in the Gulf of Aden and off Somali to ships that have minimum speeds and higher freeboards.

The chair of Lloyd's speaking on the policy of paying ransom uttered a grim warning when he commented: *At the end of the day there is no alternative if you don't want lives to be lost.* That he was speaking from an experienced viewpoint was very obvious to the shipping industry that had seen 100 ships attacked by pirates world-wide, with 39 vessels and 200 crew-members seized in 2008 alone, with an estimated total of between $30 and $80 million ransom money paid.

The problem of piracy is not new. It has been going on for some years and over these years *numerous* efforts internationally have been made to tackle the problem. Pirates board ships of all classes, from small dry-cargo or chemical coasters to deep-sea bulk carriers, container ships and supertankers, and have been known to threaten fishing vessels and large private yachts, cabin cruisers and even coastal dhows. It seems that no vessels of any particular class are guaranteed safety. Tankers fully laden with low freeboard—often around a few metres—are particularly vulnerable even to small rigid or semi-rigid craft fitted with powerful outboard motors, and manned by crews armed to the teeth. In the week that the *Sirius Star* was pirated, there were a further seven smaller ships of all classes that were hijacked—something the world's press appeared largely to overlook. The scenario until then received little media coverage and international news hounds (apart from the international maritime press) have since generally been notorious by their silence.

Reports of piracy have been highlighted, especially in the Nautilus International magazine *Telegraph*, since the 1980s focussing attention on an increasing worldwide problem, both in intensity of violence and geographical area. It seems, in a *Lloyd's Ship Manager* report supporting varying *Telegraph* reports, that attackers use an assortment of weapons ranging from rocket-propelled grenades and automatic weapons to revolvers and knives. The areas most affected include not just the notorious Gulf of Aden and Somali coast, but also Indonesia, the Malacca Straits, increasingly Nigeria, the Chinese coast, the Caribbean, and more recently Peru.

Since 2004 according to the *Telegraph*, the International Chamber of Shipping's International Maritime Board's (ICC/IMB) Piracy Reporting Centre, stated there had been a 47% increase in the number of attacks where guns had been used against seafarers, and in the first five months of that year alone, thirty seafarers had been killed. A further 125 crewmembers during this time were taken hostage and held to ransom. The previous year saw 350 seafarers' killed, 400 injured and 2,500 taken hostage on their ships indicating to the IMB the *ease with which ships can be attacked and their crews overpowered*. In the face of these horrifying statistics from 'years picked at random', indifference in some quarters comes close to callousness. Not only can piracy attacks be expected in a greater geographical area, but the pirates are extending their operations by moving considerably away from coastal waters and further out to sea.

In August 2004, the governments of flag states Indonesia, Malaysia and Singapore agreed to carry out round-the-year patrols using corvettes to combat piracy in the Malacca Straits, but later that month, the governments collectively agreed to scale down these proposals and reduce them to local waters asserting *that they would have no legal rights to pursue pirates into the territorial waters of other countries*. In the same year, a Japanese initiative established an organisation directed towards sharing information about piracy bonding sixteen Asian countries into an amalgamation that attracted support from IMO. In September 2005, for instance, IMO organised a meeting with the government of Indonesia to discuss piracy-related issues, and have since encouraged further initiatives with other nations worldwide. Regardless of these efforts (which take time to organise and implement), in Indonesia there were still 79 reported attacks during 2005. During that same year, pirate attacks were reported in a new area, when ten incidents occurred in Iraqi waters seemingly near Basrah oil terminal and Umm Qasr.

The problem is not an easy one to solve. In the many areas from which pirates operate, there are miles of isolated coastline to patrol containing a plethora of bays and islands that offer ideal hiding places and conditions. There seems to be international agreement that the pirates work spontaneously and not from any predetermined information that might permit them to target specific vessels. Over the years, United Nations Security Council involvement in proposing measures supporting flag states *whose naval vessels and military aircraft operate in international waters and airspace adjacent to the coast of Somali to be vigilant to any incident of piracy therein and to take appropriate action to protect merchant shipping.* This action was immediately followed by reports from the IMB lamenting the 'serious lack of resources available' to sustain the UNSC threat. As long ago as October 2006, the IMB launched an online map designed to help shipmasters and owners whose vessels must sail through what they termed 'piracy hot spots' and 'be better prepared for possible attacks'. Responding to a readers' survey in *LSM* conducted from December 2005 to January 2006, findings indicated amongst other points that: *Governments in the affected areas need to become involved in identifying the pirates and places where they live, and then doing something about them.* The Journal of the Honourable Company of Master Mariners reported that thc House of Commons Transport Committee had recently instituted a short enquiry into the problems of piracy on the high seas, developing reported strategies advocated in a recent edition of their magazine. The new enquiry included assessment of causality in piracy and guidelines offered by international organisations to deal with the problem. Recent regulatory implementation by IMO leading to the embossing of unique recognition numbers to ships has made positive response to the problem of ship stealing and re-sale. Following the *Sirius Star* attack, the EU and NATO working with other maritime nations agreed to reinforce the existing warships by sending up to a further ten military craft in an effort to stem the flow of this trade.

It was earlier in May 2006, following months of careful and intensive research, that IMO announced the Long Range Identification and Tracking system of ships (LRIT), a requirement under SOLAS Chapter V applying initially to passenger and cargo ships, including high-speed craft, above 300 grt travelling on international voyages. This is not to be confused with the Automatic Identification of Ships (AIS) system fitted aboard all ships exceeding 250 grt. *Tanker Operator* in its January/February 2007 issue featured an article outlining the proposed system, *"Ships engaged on international voyages have to automatically transmit data concerning the identity of the ship, its position and the date and time of that position. The main purpose of LRIT is for government agencies to use the information to enhance national security. It can also help search and rescue (SAR) co-ordinators to determine what ships are in the vicinity of a vessel in distress, particularly in areas away from coastal waters".* Provision is made for countries who do not wish involvement in the scheme (perhaps due to their low risk assessment for security means) or any other event allowing the Master of the vessel momentarily to cease transmissions for possible 'security' purposes. Two effective results of LRIT could be to deter pirates stealing any particular vessel and disposing of the crew, cargo and ship itself, and to monitor any vessel under a terrorist threat.

Some measures have been taken which, on the face of it, do not appear very effective. One is to suggest the re-routeing of ships away from the affected areas, but as the *Sirius Star* was taken 450 miles off-shore it seems that this might produce limited results, especially in the light of the larger tonnage powered pirated craft that provide criminals with their extra range. The other is a suggestion that naval personnel might be carried aboard ships during their passages within the areas, or specially trained security staff—but each would require accommodation to be found on board, something which is not always an easy task. The idea has been mooted of arming merchant seamen with automatic weapons. This has had a mixed reception, with some serving crew members in favour of the idea but—apart from some legal and insurance ramifications—the thought of 'Jolly Jack' particularly or even a trained security guard rampaging around the main deck with a loaded automatic weapon fills many others with horror.

Many proposals and moves are occurring that are positive even within their restrictions. Shipping organisations such as OCIMF (the Oil Companies International Maritime Forum) in conjunction with the IMB, Intercargo, Intertanko and SIGTTO produced in 2009 an excellent guide that contains much positive information advocating to seafarers—who are after all in the front-line of activities—practical measures to avoid, delay or deter piracy attacks. The suggestions include advising vessels to proceed at full speed across the wide range of piracy threatened areas, locking and securing thoroughly all water-tight doors with additional internal devices, and using pressurised fire hoses when convenient, safe and appropriate to do so.

Indonesia alone so far seems to have been particularly effective in reducing pirate attacks on shipping in their waters, for in the first quarter of 2009 only one incident was recorded, compared to five during the previous quarter.

The implementation of LRIT became mandatory in January 2009 with over 70 flag states becoming involved. *Tanker Oper-*

ator reported that BP Shipping, with the testing and certification of their entire fleet of 55 tankers led the world in June 2009 by becoming the first major ship-owner to be 100% compliant.

The world's navies *are* playing an important role attempting to control piracy in the Gulf of Aden, Somalian and other waters, even though the problem remains enormous owing to the vastness of the areas of water concerned. All manner of organisations have become involved. The chair of the Nippon Foundation, speaking at an IMO conference in May 2009 celebrating the twentieth anniversary of the International Maritime Law Institute (IMLI) commented on the maritime co-operation which existed when he said: *"Piracy is a scourge that affects the entire world and combating it is in the interest of the entire international community. Today, it is projected that ultimately about 40 countries will participate in fighting piracy off Somalia. I believe that never in history have so many nations come together like this for a common purpose".* Certainly, NATO forces supported by navies from a number of other countries provide warship patrols capable of launching helicopters and armed patrol vessels. They have indeed been successful in thwarting attempted hijacks. Many of the merchant ships rescued were tankers ranging from handy-sized ships to VLCCs. The problem of course is what can happen to the pirates when they are apprehended. Sometimes they try to shoot it out with the naval forces and the inevitable outcome results in their deaths. Often they are released following questioning, presumably to continue their activities. Sometimes they are arrested, and it is then open to question whether or not they can be tried for piracy under that country's own laws, or even under those of a third party—if one could be found that was able to accept this responsibility. *Tanker Operator* reported recently that *"the US has already taken legal action to establish criminal courts with the powers of prosecuting a captured pirate in New York",* and a number of governments have discussed also the possibilities of prosecuting pirates in one of the member States. The issue has been raised also that perhaps international piracy courts could be established, but these would take many years to discuss and agree before they could become established and commence functioning.

Notwithstanding these efforts and indeed successes, the problem shows little sign of diminishing off the Somali coast and Gulf of Aden. The IMB declared that by May 2009, there had been 29 successful hijackings with 114 unsuccessful attempts, with 54 instances of merchant ships being fired upon stating *'this was a considerable increase over the previous year'.*

All the time that direct political intervention seems impossible, pirates will continue to 'have their way'. Notwithstanding their attendance at international piracy conferences in Djibouti in 2009 and their request to the international maritime community for assistance to establish an effective coast-guard, Somalia has been without an effectively stable government since 1991. Ethiopian forces took over in 2006 replacing the Islamic control who had eradicated piracy by threatening to behead offenders brought before their Islamic courts. This action seemed to work very effectively. Now that measure has been withdrawn, it seems ('horror of horror' in some quarters) that it will be only by opening some form of positive direct negotiation with the current political controllers that any hope of resolution can be discovered. The perennial problem of course is how this could be established in the light of 'existing political conditions' in this country.

Closely related to issues of piracy perhaps is the potential problem of terrorism where merchant shipping is used to further evil ends. The possibilities mooted include seizing a ship —any ship, but why not a fully laden tanker—using this to block a port entrance, or even a narrow strait, perhaps offering diverse threats holding a country at ransom. Again, this issue is not a new one for, since 9/11, considerable debates have occurred in maritime and near-maritime circles regarding the vulnerability of shipping to potential threats from terrorist sources. It is interesting that 'authoritative organisations' have problems deciding whether or not the issues of piracy and terrorism should be discussed together or whether they are best left as separate entities. A former security adviser to the United States government addressing an IMB conference a couple of years ago offered a key address that defended the idea of separating the two. He suggested evidence that since the 1960s: *'there have been fewer than two hundred serious terrorist incidents in the marine environment, out of a total of 10,000 terrorist attacks around the world'.* He admitted the possibility of containers being used *'to deliver a weapon of mass destruction was an issue of significant concern'.* Nautilus UK's head of communications however, addressing the same conference, maintained that piracy and security should not be viewed separately and referred to the abysmal record in preventing the spread of piracy and armed attacks on shipping over the past two decades. This representative regarded the two issues as connected because *'the long-standing lack of action to prevent the remorseless rise in piracy has potentially opened the door to terrorism at sea'.* Because terrorist attacks directly using shipping have not occurred, it hardly represents a reasoned argument that they will not therefore occur in the future. Alarming reports, picking-up the theme expressed by the US security adviser, were recorded recently in the *Telegraph* that *'two Palestinians detonated explosives in the Israeli port of Ashdod after entering in a container with a secret compartment'.* This report serves the warning that 'what can happen once, can happen again', perhaps with a subsequently more devastating outcome. Once again, IMO have shown determination in taking initiatives to protect shipping by imposing regulations embossing a specific Ship's IMO Number on the vessel, and by introducing amendments to the STCW Codes stipulating guidance for the training and certification of ship security officers (SSOs), but the extent to which they will be carried aboard tankers has not been clarified. It was in June 2004 that they introduced also an ISPS code (International Security Programme for Ships) against terrorism offering protection to ship, crews and cargo.

Chapter Seven

Practical Insights

Electronic navigation (or 'e-nav' as it is known colloquially) is a well-established practice aboard nearly all sizes of merchant vessels, including of course most tankers. Integral to the system are computerised chart displays (ECDIS) which have been used practically at sea, backed by paper systems, since the early 1990s. There are two systems, of which the UK Hydrographic Office ARCS (Admiralty Raster Chart Service) uses scans of British Admiralty (BA prefixed) paper charts. The 3,500 or so BA charts necessary for world coverage have been digitised into facsimiles on a series of CDs that can be updated regularly by disc from traditional Admiralty Notices to Mariners. The second system uses charts produced by commercial organisations worldwide based on the geographical positions of charted coastlines and objects as vector coordinates, known as Electronic Navigation Charts (ENC). The information is obtained from paper charts of the hydrographic authorities on payment of a fee and displayed as 'layers' such that buoyage and lights or soundings may be suppressed and then reinstated at the direction of the navigating officer.

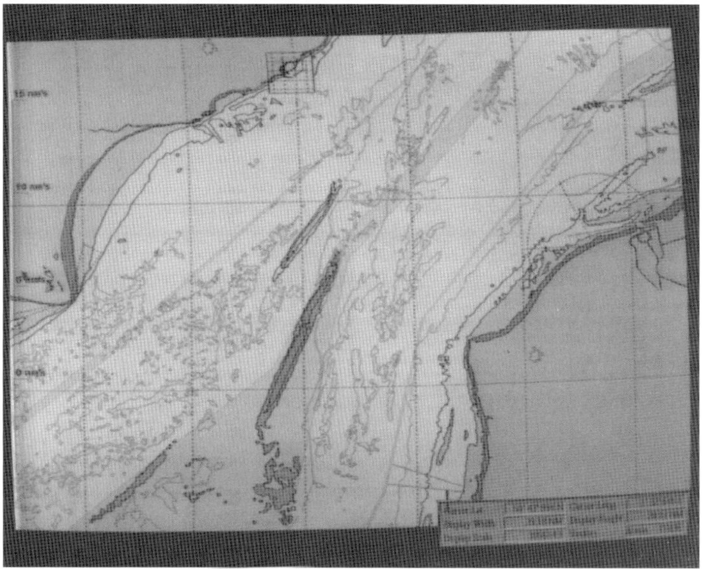

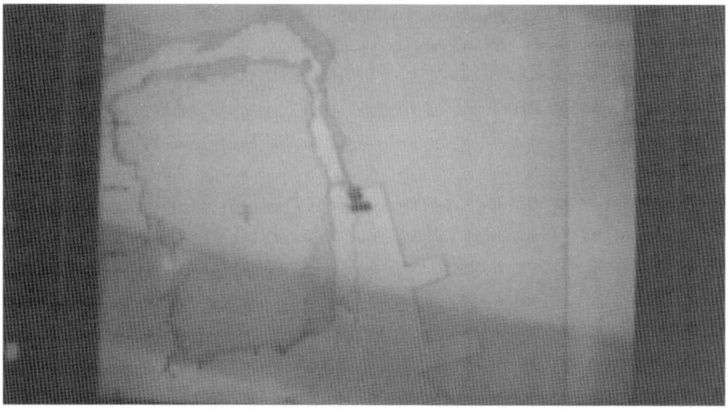

Screen shot of an electronic navigation chart (ENC) of the Dover Strait in which layers have been suppressed (which may be reinstated at any time) giving details and references to soundings, named shore identification features, lights, navigation buoys and light-vessels, leaving only salient coast outlines, sand banks and the traffic separation zones. This can be useful in areas where a number of soundings are close together and 'clutter up the screen' with too much information, at moments when depth below the keel is confirmed as safe, but attention needs to be focussed on other areas. Review and zoom facilities enable passage planning to be quick and effective. (Racal-Decca Marine).

The 'zoom' facility on electronic chart systems is effective and practically useful as demonstrated here by the showing of a large vessel closing her berth in restricted waters. This facility is available in any condition of visibility (Racal-Decca Marine).

I recall using the ENC version of ECDIS for the first time whilst visiting Transas Marine, a major player among electronic systems providers then based in Southampton. During this visit I planned a theoretical VLCC passage from Coryton in the River Thames to Mena al Ahmadi in the Arabian Gulf (a familiar routeing of days gone by, still used today) in around thirty minutes. The overall planning was initially worked on small-scale charts, following which a chronological succession of larger-scale ones enabled completion through the use of waypoints relating to subsequent legs of the passage, in a similar way to the system explained as a practical operation aboard *British Ensign*, but extended worldwide. The process was much in the manner of 'traditional' methods using paper charts only, that would have been worked in 'legs' over a voyage, which proved highly labour intensive so far as the second officer was concerned. Using ECDIS and 'paper charts only' still requires reference to supporting publications such as routeing instructions, weather forecasts, Admiralty lists of lights—and pilots for the areas, tidal stream information, etc all of which are available today electronically. For years now both paper and the two computerised systems have been used simultaneously and a demonstration to this effect was made as long ago as 1997 aboard a container ship—the *Katrine Maersk*. Regarding this voyage, the United Kingdom Hydrographic Office (UKHO) announced, 'The demonstration uses official ENC (vector) data in the critical harbour areas of Singapore and Hong Kong and their approaches, with Admiralty (raster) charts linking the two across the China Sea. The combined use of official vector and raster charts is a major step forward in marine safety.' During 2008, IMO under SOLAS Chapter V governing the safety of navigation drafted regulations to make mandatory the carriage of ECDIS for ships engaged on international voyages. For tankers, the regulations govern those ships of 3,000 grt and upwards constructed on or after a proposed date of 1 July 2012, although this does not of course preclude the fitting of systems prior to this date.

My research found rather limited evidence, in the midst of wider acclamation, that not all ECDIS software is up to the mark, especially when some systems are used. The navigation superintendent of a major shipowner, a professional seafarer, gave a number of warnings about ECDIS in an article for *Safety at Sea International*. He evoked a recent incident when a ship grounded and commented: '...the pilot made his decision based on an unofficial system and he touched bottom as a result.' The answer, he suggested, was 'for complete ENC chart coverage to be made compulsory'. Amongst other incidents, he cited a case when Traffic Separation Zone layers 'went missing' and suggested some individual Hydrographic offices and regional ENC coordinating centres, and indeed firms themselves, are operating from commercial motives regarding distribution rights. Where the ECDIS system is official he suggested that it is more effective than using paper charts largely because the chart is on the screen in front of the navigator and, again, negates the necessity for him or her to have to make an extra visit to the chartroom or a behind the screen table. A further article in the same magazine commented on the mixed verdicts relating to ECDIS performance as monitored by officers aboard the ships using the system. 'The one thing that everyone seemed to agree on was that when ECDIS is working properly, it's brilliant. The navigating officer knows exactly where the ship is, he can judge what other ships are likely to do, passage planning is easier and chart updates are the work of minutes. Unfortunately, when something goes wrong it can have an impact that can be out of proportion to the problem itself.'

Certainly, the mailing of Notices to Mariners 'in the old days' left much to be desired, with sometimes a ship leaving port for a long-haul passage without up-to-date corrections. This is not a problem with ECDIS, but the system does have other difficulties unique to computerisation. Amongst those mentioned has been the crashing of hard discs due to vibration, with solid-state hard drives suggested as possible antidotes. A new positional system called EPDIS is currently under trial based on three-dimensional geodetic information provided by satellite and laser surveys combined with object data from current pilot books, maps and charts. The acronym stands for Electronic Pilot Display Information System and is an interactive, dynamic visualisation for the navigating officer, offering not only the electronic chart, but on a different adjacent screen, a visual image of the coastline as seen from the bridge. The advantage promoted advocates a continuous visual image regardless of fog or during dark night hours. Currently, in its experimental stage, it seems likely to be restricted to coastal and pilotage use.

Generally, however, the way ahead looks promising; the implementation of new strategies to ease the burden of the navigating officer will inevitably lead to safer navigation systems. These allow for the adoption of new digital improvements which are sufficiently flexible to take on board new programs as these become available.

A raft of additional legal requirements continue to be reviewed by IMO leading to safer and more efficient ships, including such items as Voyage Data Recorders (VDR) operational aboard tankers of responsible owners for many years now which act as equivalents of the 'black box' on aircraft. Most modern tankers have been fitted or retrofitted with mandatory emergency towing equipment. To comply with 1996 amendments to the Safety of Life at Sea (SOLAS) Convention, 'safe access to the tanker bow from the accommodation' has to be provided across the upper deck in the form of a traditional 'catwalk', and tankers have to be fitted with mooring systems conforming to OCIMF Mooring Equipment Guidelines. Other improvements incorporate carbon dioxide (CO_2) being used instead of Halon as the fire-extinguishing agent for the engine- and pump-rooms. And all tankers are now mandatorily equipped with a water-spray fitted lifeboat, whether davit launched or stern-launched free-fall types. The provision of fast rescue boats (FRB) is a legal requirement as well as the provision of satisfactory lifejacket and immersion gear, as demonstrated in the previous chapter.

It is right that the familiar traditional open lifeboat, fitted to all tankers on the port and starboard sides forward of the accommodation block, should be replaced by totally enclosed craft. As observed aboard both tankers during the voyages, a tanker with average crew numbers of 25 requires a lifeboat some 7.5 metres in length x 2.75 m x 3.42 m, with all personnel facing aft to ensure increased safety, apart from the controlling officer. Free-fall lifeboats initially experienced a few problems, which have been confronted by legislation imposed by IMO, and the introduction of fail-safe off-load/on-load lifeboat release systems which provide the safe launch and retrieval of lifeboats lowered from davits. These systems must conform also to the requirements of SOLAS and LSA codes.

The open life-boat served older generations of tankers for many years notwithstanding its limitations regarding exposure to the elements and when leaving a blazing ship. Basically, the boat was all that there was and it was accepted in that light (Author's Collection).

A thirty-foot covered lifeboat carried at the stern of a modern tanker of the 'free fall' type offers a safe and secure method of leaving a ship during an emergency. The officer in charge is in the enclosed cock-pit whilst the remainder of the crew sit facing aft (Author's Collection).

Close-up of free fall lifeboat (Author's Collection).

The fast rescue boat (FRB) carried by all tankers is to assist a person or ship in distress. The FRB is launched from a single hook and in practical use would probably be launched whilst the parent tanker itself is under way, which assists the launch by controlling the swing of the FRB as it is lowered. Difficulties were originally experienced with the hook, although these have since been satisfactorily resolved.

A fast rescue boat used for the recovery of individuals either from 'man overboard' situations on the parent tanker, or from situations involving the rescue of survivors from other ships. The launching crane can be seen in the background. The boat invariably is used for a multitude of purposes related to the ordinary practices aboard as well as for training purposes (Author's Collection and V. Volden).

In recent years, considerable attention has been paid to practices in some countries of ship recycling involving running the vessel at full speed onto a beach at high water and, as the tide ebbs, bringing crews of labourers and semi-skilled workers to dismantle the vessel by saws and torches 'as she sits'.

A popular Sunday colour supplement in the United Kingdom a few years ago gave extensive coverage to this practice, thus bringing it to the notice of the general public. The work occasionally hits the international press—particularly when a spate of accidents focusses the world's attention. I recall talking to a serving ship's master who had returned recently from running his ship onto one such beach. His bemused expression and the rueful smile crossing his countenance reflected both delight and consternation as he obeyed his owners' demands and 'put his redundant supertanker on the putty at Alang' in southern India—a complete antithesis to professional training and practices of a lifetime at sea. The problem is still of disturbing proportions. Ship recycling enabling *all* parts of ships to be reused is environmentally sound in principle, but the safety of working practices involved here are highly questionable. The *Telegraph* advised recently: '95% of old ships are broken up and recycled on the beaches of Bangladesh, India, China, Pakistan and Turkey. In the most appalling conditions—often earning less than a dollar a day—ship-breaking workers in these countries face such hazards as fire, explosions, falls from great heights, and exposure to asbestos, heavy metals and PVCs.'

As a result also of increasing public interest and concerns, IMO have pressed for regulations making this practice safer and more efficient. In 2003, they adopted Guidelines on Ship Recycling, with recommendations relating to safety, and in 2005 IMO's Marine Environment Protection Committee (MEPC) agreed that IMO should become directly involved by implementing legally enforced regulations. Later MEPC meetings confronted concerns on other maritime issues, but resolved to push for implementation of a mandatory shipping instrument subjecting ship recycling to environmentally safe operational practices. This went a step further than facilitating eventual disposal of classes of ships because it incorporated facets of design, construction and operation. The idea suggested regulatory procedures to encompass shipping from already rigidly supervised construction, through life time stages eventually to recycling. Moves towards this action have since been implemented at IMO's MSC meetings which recommended introducing goal-based standards for shipbuilding. The final stages, spread over a number of years, would result in rigid control and reporting requirements. In anticipation of IMO's action, India announced a health and safety regime effective from December 2006. *Fairplay* reported how the Indian Supreme court had 'found one in six workers at Alang is suffering from asbestosis as a result of poor handling and disposal of asbestos on ships'. The country has 'bitten the bullet' on this issue because India announced it was introducing procedures designed to enforce a rigid health and safety regime planned to cover other aspects of ship-breaking. As the magazine concluded, after recounting a number of tragic human stories: 'if ship breaking disappears as an industry in India, then regrettably that is preferable to allowing further misery, illness and death.'

Whilst considerable advances have been made, and continue to be made, to improve safety, ship breaking on some Indian and Pakistani beaches remains a source of danger to the personnel involved (Brian Entwistle).

CHAPTER EIGHT

The Proactive Approach

It was during the April 2005 Intertanko Athens Tanker Conference that decisions were made of potentially monumental significance. A unique gathering of leading influential and authoritative members representing the wider shipping and allied industries met with an agreed determination to address and break many deadlocks mentioned in the previous chapters. Under the impressive ruins of the Temple of Poseidon—appropriately the Greek god of the sea—concerns were aired over the stance taken by the tanker industry towards tanker accidents and incidents. Inevitably, issues were raised surrounding the raft of past, present and future legislation, regulating further the operation of crude oil and product-carrying ships. Even if the emphasis of this gathering was necessarily partially introspective nobody could accuse them of retrospective thinking, for from their deliberations emerged a new and bold philosophy which, on the face of things, appeared of seemingly preposterous import. Up until 2005 the tanker industry had taken a stance seeking solutions based retrospectively on events. In other words they had *reacted*. The argument presented itself that perhaps more objective results could occur were the industry to consider a *proactive* stance, agree on the course the action should take, then implement it through a new spirit of conciliatory proposals. Groups including shipping companies, people engaged in oil transportation across all levels and others involved in a range of supporting professions—each of whom had previously worked individually—should set new goals of excellence, and work *collectively* to achieve these. From such constructive thinking was born the Poseidon Challenge.

Perhaps a seminal idea had grown from the violent reactions of both media and industry to the shock of the *Erika* and *Prestige* disasters, for it was about this time that the chairman of a leading tanker company, Maritrans, quietly challenged rightful outcries in asserting the belief that zero pollution *was* capable of being achieved. He proceeded to put such revolutionary views into practice with his own tanker fleet. His message was simple. 'Not one drop' of oil should seep, leak or overflow from his ships. To the surprise of silent critics and a more than casually interested industry, his fleet have subsequently experienced infinitesimal spills. These figures included the usually inevitable casual deck spillage out of the 7 billion-plus gallons, or 24 million tons of crude oil and products carried by Maritrans each year. The fleet was involved in about 2,000 cargo operations each year, which works out at around five per day. In November 2005, the Poseidon Challenge took this achievement a stage further. In a drive for excellence, as a sign to the man in the street internationally that the oil tanker business 'was meaning business', Intertanko paralleled a plan amongst their members to strive for 'zero fatalities—zero pollution—and zero ship detentions'. As the chairman of Intertanko stated, 'The primary purpose of the Poseidon Challenge, and its meaningful and realistic goal, is to look back in 5 years (2010) and see serious accidents and fatalities reduced to zero, accident and pollution rates reduced to zero and port state control detentions reduced to zero.' As Intertanko readily asserted, 'it took effort and courage to get agreement on this proactive approach. But as the tanker industry takes its future into its own hands, it welcomes the support received from the wider shipping industry for the concept of the "zero" goals.'

The assumption was made that shared goals are achievable only by integrated voluntary efforts whereby the industry itself sets high standards for performance rather than relying purely on governmental or environmental regulators. It was fervently believed that success could indeed be achieved—but only by implementing a long-term strategy extended across the whole of the tanker industry. The policy was extremely far-sighted, as it foresaw Intercargo members including dry bulk carriers, container ships and cargo vessels to involve ultimately the entire shipping industry. As a next step, all subscribing participants pledged to weld themselves into a 'chain of responsibility' consisting of 15 links working together with sustained commitment to achieve the continued programme of improvements. Essentially, everyone would have to participate. Subscribing components of the chain included agents, bunker providers, hull and P&I insurance, flag and port States, classification societies, equipment providers, seafarers, those in the ship construction and demolition industries, everyone involved in delivering quality recruitment and training, and all ship owner-managers and operators. These groups between them cover terminals, pilotage and towage, waterways navigable by seagoing tankers, repair groups and salvors.

Intertanko's contribution was considerably more involved than the role of coordinating member groups and undertaking logistics for planning future conferences, for it offered a responsible lead concerning the final outcomes of deliberations. Firstly they would ensure that the way forward conformed strictly to internationally adopted rules and regulations by monitoring negotiations present and future across relevant international organisations. Secondly, they encouraged rapid ratification, uniform implementation and enforcement of the relevant international conventions. Thirdly, they agreed a commitment establishing a Human Factors working committee to develop equal technical capability in this sector.

The question of all flag states accepting their responsibilities in full—and *being seen* to do so—was recognised as a major contributory factor to the success of Poseidon negotiations. Efficient tankers operate only where flag states inspect all ships and *effectively* examine operating standards to ensure they conform to international IMO safety and anti-pollution measures. As examined in this book, a few flag states continue to turn a seemingly blind eye by cloaking deficiencies and passing ships that elsewhere would fail inspections and be classified as substandard. If Poseidon ideals were to succeed, then all such ships had to be eliminated, and working this process in reverse, all flag states had to be open to examination audits. The proactive approach suggested by Intertanko encouraged a *voluntary* system of audit as the positive way forward to support those who were foundering. It was a subtle suggestion for it placed the onus of conforming squarely onto the shoulders of those countries. Any flag state not then conforming would focus attention directly upon itself and emerge as conspicuously as the proverbial lighthouse on a dark night. If this could only be made to work, then a major step forward would have been taken, defusing Dr Ladyman's 'more in anger than reality tongue-in-cheek notion' of invasion (see p.110). The Organisation asserted its stand in direct and unequivocal language: '(We are) strongly in favour of flag state audit recommendations being implemented and also being made public. We will work only with flags which do undergo an audit, which do make these findings public, and which do implement the recommendations.' The gauntlet had been thrown down and the onus placed upon all flag states to 'consider their position'.

Reaction to the Poseidon Challenge from associated organisations was enthusiastic and totally supportive. The secretary-general of IMO commended particularly the robust and visionary approach moulding all groups into the 15-linked chain: 'But delivering the oil around the world without a drop being spilled depends on more than just the tanker operator. It depends on all those whose activity touches on a ship during its voyage—from broker and charterer to pilot and oil terminal, from builder and classification society to insurer and salvor. For a shipping accident can be triggered by any one of the links in the chain of responsibility—and a chain is only as strong as its weakest link.' He pledged that he and his colleague member states would continue 'developing and implementing, as appropriate, the regulations, guidelines and recommendations that will assist the maritime community in achieving the goals of zero fatalities, zero pollution and zero detentions through continuous improvement.' Unequivocal support also came from major sources including the ITOPF, European Maritime Safety Agency (EMSA), the International Association of Ports and Harbours (IAPH), as well as flag-state secretariats and port state control organisations.

Positive actions from delegates involved in the chain of responsibility were promised immediately, and in the seven-month period from formulating resolves, a series of commitments were clarified, promulgated and enacted. The range was impressive and exhaustive. The President of the Federation of National Associations of Shipbrokers and Agents (FONASBA) agreed 'to survey their members so we can tell you which ports have slop facilities and good waste reception facilities'. The Secretary-General of the International Bunker Industry Association (IBIA) committed to an 'Improvement in the measurement for bunkering quantity metering and the monitoring of the sulphur content.' The Chairman of the International Association of Classification Societies (IACS) singled out 'a small number of key initiatives' —numbering six major measures, especially extending their assistance 'to poorly performing flag-States'. The Senior Member of The International Union of Marine Insurance's Cargo Committee made four commitments including how to 'explore ways to share information on substandard vessels'. Six measures were promised by the President of the International Salvage Union (ISU), with ITF making four commitments, and the President of Videotel asserting the intention of his organisation to 'to provide seafarers with the training tools they need to be kept abreast of shipboard technology and its changes.'

The determination agreed in 2005 did not lie dormant. For in the following April the first Poseidon Challenge Conference occurred in Singapore, attended by 250 top executives from the 15 link organisations in the emergent chain. As Intertanko mentioned: 'Some started the day off wondering what it was all about. By the end of the day nobody was left in any doubt.' Participants had bestowed upon them authority to support Poseidon concepts, aims and ideals—and to forge these into feasibly tangible and realistic commitments that would lead to continuous improvements and achieve the threefold zero policy intentions. As reported by Intertanko, 'all pledged to be part of this bid to make the industry what we all want it to be. Firm, realisable commitments were made, both by the invited speakers and by those participating from the floor'. The chairman reviewed progress made over the previous year and, in already looking forward to the next Challenge Day fixed for March 2007 in Istanbul, emphasised how such realistic commitment could be envisaged: 'It's about improving the way we run our businesses. We need to have people here who really want to be here, who want to make a difference. Basically, it's all about changing what we do. *If you do what you did, then you get what you got.*' Perhaps the aphorism of the final comment reached the heart of the conference in the support offered by another speaker, the president of Teekay Marine Services, Teekay Shipping (Canada). He not only stressed the need for enthusiasm but reinforced the necessity of changing current practices where these had been examined and found wanting. He also spelled out what commitment means in practical terms, and offered his own aphorism for delegates to take on board, 'Poseidon Challenge is an obsessive and sustained commitment to best practices, a willingness to embrace change, an openness and desire to learn from our mistakes... Ultimately, if it is not supported by time, energy, money and passion, it won't work. *We have to walk the talk.*' The impressive factor is the aggression behind the intent. It is as if delegates 'put their money where their mouth is' in a determined effort *wanting* positive action by identifying areas of weakness and addressing these to bring about the envisaged threefold zero changes. Supporting the intent of the March 2006 Challenge Day and seeking not to 'hide a collective light under the proverbial bushel', Intertanko screened complete details of their vision on their website and then introduced publication of the achievements to the media, 'in a constructive yet relaxed atmosphere with so many journalists who know the shipping industry well'.

In 2008 Intertanko reviewed actions in which it had been involved over the preceding years—a period of particularly active negotiations, each furthering the ideals of Poseidon. The organisation continued fighting against regional non-federal and international regulation in the United States and elsewhere with some notable successes, following the winning of their important legal battle in 2000 (seen in Chapter Four) when the state of Washington was ordered by the US Supreme Court to stop enforcing its own laws affecting the manning of tankers, and their design and operations. In June 2006, the State of Massachusetts was permanently enjoined by the local American District Court from enforcing their Oil Spill Prevention Act with the court declaring the statute unconstitutional and accusing the State of trying to make laws in areas reserved exclusively to the Federal Government. This decision upheld the regulatory authority of the US Coast Guard over ship operations in American waters, preventing local legislation pre-empting federal regulations. Related ongoing situations include challenges to the State of California's Air Resources Board (CARB) who wish to impose more rigid air emission standards than those permitted by the federal government. An EU Directive on Ship Source Pollution which sought to criminalise accidental pollution *from whatever cause* within EU member state territorial waters was a further example of regional regulation 'being at odds' with international rulings. The intransigence contained within this stringent ruling involved Intertanko and a broad coalition of other agencies—including Intercargo, Lloyd's Register, the Greek Shipping Cooperation Committee, ISU, with positive support from numerous organisations—taking a case to the London High Court through the Secretary of State for Transport. The decision was reached in June 2006 that the 'shipping industry's arguments against the legality of the EU Directive were well founded' and a comprehensive list of issues was referred to the European Court of Justice in Luxembourg for a hearing and decision.

The EU's Third Maritime Safety Package has led to discussions on a range of extensive and far-reaching matters between Intertanko and Europe. These include vessel traffic monitoring and information systems, which incorporate the urgent need for an independent authority in all coastal states to deal with ships in distress and places of refuge, such that an *Erika* incident—where a distressed ship was shunted from port to port—should never again occur. On the very pressing subject of accident investigation, it was urged that clearer distinctions be made between technical accident investigations and criminal investigations, urging that a more positive role in this area be found for the European Maritime Safety Agency (EMSA). Items amongst other negotiations include issues of flag-state compliance, requesting member states to comply with the international standards to which they agreed when signing up with IMO, port state control and obligations of ship inspections, and how classification societies might have strengthened controls. On the question of civil liberty and financial guarantees of shipowners, Intertanko has pressed for ratification of a number of major issues covering insurance, compensation and oil spill liability.

Reinforcing further ideals of Poseidon, more proposals were submitted to the IMO/BLG working group for their consideration that have made positive contributions. Not only was their suggestion for sulphur emission reductions in fuel oil used to power tanker main engines reinforced, but also the implication was conveyed that a new design of main engine might be needed that would meet forecast tighter regulations on emissions from ships in the future. They proposed a more open debate at international levels that would be more effective in identifying the best long-term solutions for reducing air pollution. Amongst their concerns was the wider dissemination of responsibility so that the 'full burden of responsibility is not placed solely on the owner, ship and ship's staff'. In April 2007, IMO and its BLG working party were widely applauded for the swiftness of their actions in keeping Annex VI on track, by not allowing the issue to become sidetracked, so enforcing the implementation date of 2010. Even more encouraging were sounds heard in mid-2007 from America and China—arguably the world's greatest culprits—hinting at their intent to consider grappling with problems of adverse environmental emissions. The significance of their intent has placed this concern at the top of the international political agenda, but without cynicism the question is begged regarding how long it will be before positive action results.

Concerns were examined in Chapter Five regarding problems arising from anti-fouling paints protecting the external hull of ships. By January 2007, just one year before the conforming deadline, only 17 out of 166 IMO member states had ratified the Convention, leading the Secretary General of IMO, and

Intertanko with support from a number of non-governmental organisations, to encourage member states to implement the convention without further delay. Although many leading paint manufacturers stopped producing TBT-based paints (tributyltin, an aggressive biocide) around 2004, a stockpile of these harmful coatings exists that continues to be used. Certainly, until January 2008 this practice was not illegal, but so far as the essence of the Convention is concerned, it certainly remained unethical and highlighted some of the 'tip of the iceberg' problems confronting those who wish the shipping industry to be regarded in the best possible light by the man in the street. It is not only the industry that ends up with egg on its face from such rebels, but also the reputation of IMO, with something of a knock-on effect on flag states. Such actions adversely affect the good name held by the majority of responsible shipowners who have already proactively adhered to the spirit of the Convention.

Enforcement of the new legislation in 2008 also carried its own crop of difficulties, because paint testing and sampling is not a part of the duties of port state control officers. It is perhaps too glib at present to suggest it be made so, but inevitably some kind of positive attention will become necessary. Intertanko have commented on this issue: 'The EU would like to see entry by force into the IMO Convention. So would the shipping industry. And so would our rapidly changing world where society's expectations are moving ahead apace and will simply no longer accept the damaging effects of TBT on shellfish and on other marine life. This foot dragging by IMO member states is ruining all the efforts of those responsible and proactive members of the shipping industry who have already taken action.' Shipowners, the IMO, regulatory advisory bodies and all concerned with advancing the Poseidon Challenge recognise they can provide the best possible state-of-the-art technology and create rafts of legislation, but these efforts will only be as efficient as the seagoing personnel who operate them.

Chapter Six also examined briefly ongoing concerns in the shipping industry regarding officer recruitment and retention, and highlighted problems associated with fraudulent practices on the part of some nationals to obtain STCW qualifications. Reference was made to the work of international insurance brokers to encourage higher standards amongst officers and crews. These measures were part of that industry's commitment to Poseidon.

Intertanko established a Human Element in Shipping committee that met formally for the first time in January 2007 in London. The intention of the committee was to focus on proactive efforts reviewing each of these concerns: 'to promote the availability, training and utilisation of personnel with the highest quality marine skills and competencies; to achieve compliance with rules and regulations; to assist in the development of measures that highlight the role of the human element in safe, secure and environmentally sound tanker transportation; and in leading the continuous improvement of the tanker industry's performance.' Clearly their brief remains wide-ranging and comprehensive for it will entail investigation into reasons why highly intelligent youngsters with superior educational qualifications, who traditionally make the best officers, too often look elsewhere for career satisfaction. The industry worldwide needs such intelligent and dedicated young people and will have to offer comparable conditions of employment if they are to be attracted to an industry which by its very nature necessitates periods away from home, families and desired environments. Intertanko members are committed to a planned programme of officer training 'that will safeguard the tanker industry of the future'. This includes providing cadet berths as a matter of course on all new ship-buildings, improving the environment in which a minimum of perhaps two cadets per ship could serve where suitable accommodation already exists, and to provide sound academic and professional training programmes. It must always be remembered that many junior and senior shore positions in almost every branch of the shipping and tanker industry are ideally served by recruiting ex-mariners, men and women who have seagoing experience and advanced qualifications. It is only by having such skilled people in the first place that these responsible posts ashore may be competently filled. It must not of course be forgotten that every seagoing vessel, not just tankers, requires qualified and experienced masters, chief engineers and attendant officers and crews.

It was in 2008 that the Human Element in Shipping Committee of Intertanko, working closely with Warsash Maritime Academy and the Malaysian Maritime Academy, introduced the Tanker Officers Training Scheme (TOTS) to develop training standards aboard this class of ship above the requirements of STCW. This boldly positive initiative is designed to improve a spate of recent 'niggles' in failures of safety across a range of areas, and to help charterers make assessments by setting enhanced tanker industry standards. These cover officer competences, taking onboard and shore-based simulation training into consideration, and the recording of time that officers have spent both in their rank and with individual companies. Situation awareness, planning and decision making, communications and teamwork are assessed along with important elements of emotional climate and stress, commercial/organisational and moral pressures, fatigue and occupational health and safety training. Individual officer assessment is by completion of a Training Record Book (TRB) containing module-assessed shipboard tasks that have to be verified and offering details of the time spent aboard ship and with the company in any deck or engineering rank. A second part shows an officer's familiarity with company procedures, safety systems, maintenance programmes and security. There is also a computer-based assessment consisting of a CD-ROM containing 2000 multiple-choice questions covering tasks within the rank and senior positions. Thus TOTS also prepares officers for their next step up in promotion. It could be argued that because the second part of the system requires officers new to companies to commence learning their specific procedures from scratch, recruitment of experienced officers from other companies might suffer, but this remains open with the present stages of the scheme.

There have been other proactive initiatives that have resulted directly from Poseidon helping develop the raising of standards into a reality. Intertanko has made representations with classification societies designed to break deadlocks of confidentiality and insularity between some individual societies. Germane to these are issues related to information sharing on early-warning systems aimed at releasing for mutually confidential benefit information on serious structural, engine-room and equipment failures. This would identify more readily ships that are potentially substandard, preventing, for example, hull failures of the type that have led to serious pollution incidents. Other issues confronted include measures to raise the profile of IMO's forthcoming Ship Recycling Convention and speed up the process of ratification before the adoption of this Convention in 2009. This will address many of the issues related in Chapter Six, particularly as the deadline approaches for the disposal of many single-hulled tankers, enabling these to be recycled in safer conditions for workers.

A study in 2007 by Intertanko discovered there had been *substantial* reductions in tanker incidents covering a range of causes over the preceding year 2006. Collisions between tankers and other ships fell from 88 to just 9. Groundings were reduced from 46 to 8, fire and explosions, with incidents involving hull and machinery, were down from 70 to 13, and miscellaneous causes including hostile action reduced from 33 to 4. Some 40% of the few incidents occurred during arrivals and departures whilst on passage in rivers, canals or port entrances. It is interesting that only 7 incidents occurred in tankers exceeding 100,000 s-dwt (with million-barrel capacity plus) and only 10 tankers built since 2000 were involved. There is no room for complacency in these figures. Indeed that factor does not enter into an Intertanko equation determined to achieve zero toleration of accidents and pollution. Neither was any rejoicing felt regarding the 40 seafarers reported killed or missing during the 36 reported accidents.

Conclusion

All of my own observations, discussions ashore and research indicate that the tanker industry approaches the future exhibiting a refreshing air of quiet optimism. The two voyages proved essential not merely for my own updating of knowledge but for the way in which practical experience demonstrated the enthusiasm of all officers and ratings met aboard for adherence to safety and environmental protection. I did not know all of the questions I would need to ask before undertaking the two voyages for so much had altered and improved since my own deep-sea days. The 'extra' issues arose directly from my trips on the *Anna Knutsen* and *British Ensign* and the eagerness of all seagoing personnel encountered to answer my questions openly and frankly. It was the quietly unobtrusive dedication to performing a job well and efficiently exhibited by all concerned that really captured the ethos of voyages made aboard the two tankers. The voyages were refreshing in those respects. They proved important from another angle.

Finding inadequate answers on board meant that discussions had to be negotiated ashore with leading authoritative figures in all of the major organisations mentioned in these chapters. My subsequent discussions and reading indicated the wholehearted support being offered those 'at the sharp end' aboard tankers by all involved in regulatory and advisory capacities ashore. I found few illusions about the rate of future progress, for all associated organisations know the way ahead will not be easy. The promises contained in the genuine zeal surrounding the Poseidon Challenge, for example, will not be achieved in five minutes, but if steps instituted to date are any yardstick then neither will it be a 'five-minute wonder'.

The expectations are high, anticipating realistic progress across a range of ambitions. However, it would be impossible —and impracticable—for all concerns examined in chapters four to seven to be addressed, with proposals suggested and implemented within the space of one, or even a few years. It is as well to be reminded of the Poseidon pledge of 'looking back in five years' and then in 2010 judging the entire philosophy of the challenge to see what positive steps have been achieved during that period. To underpin this intent, and make it realistic, is the essence of these annual conferences.

I was left with a profound impression that the man in the street, including non-seafarers ashore, can be reassured concerning the safe and efficient operation of crude oil tankers. Oil does indeed remain in the ship and the same ships are properly and effectively handled whilst on passage and alongside either at terminals or during ship-to-ship oil transfers. The regulations are in place. These are being observed from the most junior rating to the most senior officer. It is not merely 'lip service' that is being paid, but there exists genuine desire to perform all tasks well within the raft of legislations provided to prevent accidents between ships at sea and oil spillage. My voyages also revealed the essence of what it means to be a seafarer aboard oil tankers today and gave insight into the norms of the ways of life experienced. The shore-side research was daunting and uncovered legalities and niceties of issues which cannot be solved overnight. As I suspected, there were indeed few surprises and I was left with the distinct feeling that all I could do, within my limitations as an ex-mariner, would be to give the issues an airing.

By the same author

Mariner's Launch

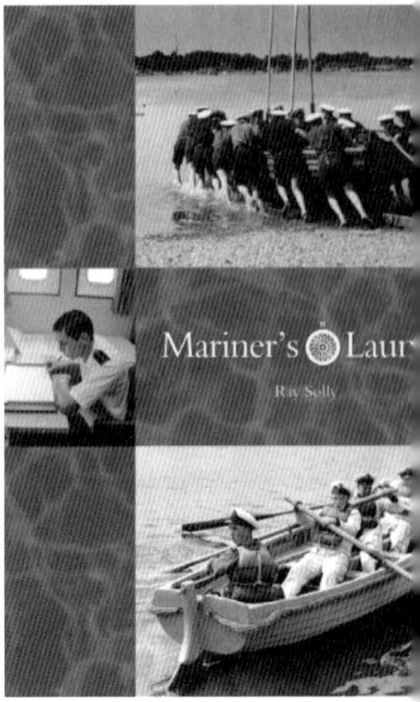

A social and historical narrative depicting life in the British Merchant Navy during the 1950s – the golden age of shipping

'This book presents a rich tapestry of life at sea in a bygone era and at the same time provides an important historical record of our country's maritime heritage.' *Commodore R.W. Warwick, Master, Queen Mary 2*

Mariner's Launch chronicles the early career of a naïve 16-year-old, Jonathan Caridia, and his development into a mature young man, capable of accepting the grave responsibilities entrusted to a watch-keeping officer on the bridge of an ocean-going ship. The reader follows his voyage escapades and sees him ambushed by pitfalls resulting largely from his innocence. These incidents capture the atmosphere of service as a navigating officer cadet in yesterday's Merchant Navy – a lifestyle which epitomised excitement and adventure during this 'golden age' of international shipping, and where young people were expected to meet the demanding everyday challenges.

'Ray Solly translates his observations into a record of moments of madness, danger, companionship and hilarity known to all who went to sea in the post war period. ...don't miss this book, it really did happen this way.' *Sea Breezes*

ISBN 1-904445-03-9 240 × 170 mm
numerous photographs softback £1

Mariner's Voy

ISBN 978-1904445-50-0 240 × 170 mm
208pp liberally illustrated softback £16.99

Jonathan's adventures continue in the second volume in the trilogy capturing life on board sea-going ships during the 1960s

... Dr. Solly has very cleverly woven together a social history of seafaring post-war years... a wonderfully evocative read, and an important contrib to the history of the period.

Extract from the Foreword by John F. Millican, Dir
Warsash Maritime Academy, Southampt

Having left behind his cadetship, Jonathan joins, with some trepidatio first vessel as Third Navigating Officer. Still in the 'golden days' of seaf the narrator relates the significant economic and social changes of the providing an insight into a way of life now overtaken by events.

'...the companionship that seafarers enjoyed from being in each c company served them well and this book proves that going to sea was u an exciting life. ...thanks are due to the author for recording those tim posterity. ... a book not to be missed.' *Sea Breezes*

'A UNIQUE narrative ...that helps capture the total experience of being a ... The book not only seeks to present the variety of duties comprising a officer's work, but also explores the effect upon his attitude of mind of the personalities, aboard and ashore, he encounters along with the impact extraordinary events that overtake his ship from time to time. A very sati account of merchant ship seafaring of the day.' *Nautical Magazine*

Whittles Publishing • Dunbeath Mains Cottages • Dunbeath • KW6 6EY • UK
Tel: +44 (0)1593-731 333 • Fax: +44(0)1593-731 400
e-mail: info@whittlespublishing.com www.whittlespublishing.com